A BASKETFUL OF BROKEN DISHES

A *a true story* BASKETFUL *of* BROKEN DISHES

Naomi Mullet Stutzman

AMBASSADOR INTERNATIONAL
GREENVILLE, SOUTH CAROLINA & BELFAST, NORTHERN IRELAND

www.ambassador-international.com

A Basketful of Broken Dishes

Printed in the United States of America

ISBN: 9781935507680

Cover Design & Page Layout by David Siglin

First printing: August 2011
Second printing: October 2011

AMBASSADOR INTERNATIONAL
Emerald House
427 Wade Hampton Blvd.
Greenville, SC 29609, USA
www.ambassador-international.com

AMBASSADOR BOOKS
The Mount
2 Woodstock Link
Belfast, BT6 8DD, Northern Ireland, UK
www.ambassador-international.com

The colophon is a trademark of Ambassador

In Memory of

Simon & Susan Mullet

Dorothy Mullet Leonard

Dedicated to

My loving family

Table of Contents

Appreciation & Special Thanks

My Heavenly Father for all the gentle whispers that kept me going. I don't even know how to express my gratitude, except to give my life to You. May the plans You have for me become my dreams. Praise, thanks, and honor to You, my Lord and Savior, Jesus Christ!

Doyle—the love of my life, my engineer husband, for bringing an old computer home from work and insisting that I learn to use it before computers were even in homes. Thanks for always keeping me running smoothly. What a blessing to always have a computer tech on call 24/7. Without you this book would have never been written. God knew I needed you to complete the plans He had for me.

Brothers and sisters—Atlee, Kathy, Betty, and Fred for showing me love and kindness all my life. You helped form what I am today. We have gone through some difficult times together, but we are better for it. Love you more than you may know.

Yvonne, my daughter, for saying something so profound after hearing the story about her grandparents, that I used it in my book.

Monica, my daughter who lives across the country but was always available when I needed her opinion. She also seemed to know exactly when her mother needed a word from the Lord and it was exactly what I needed to hear.

Cousin Joe for all the stories he knew about my father. God brought you into our lives at the right time. What a blessing you were, in more ways than one.

Barb and Andy, my first cousins, for answering my many questions. Meeting you was an answer to prayer.

Peggy Hearl for giving me the title to this book and always believing in me.

Claire Gritman for being with me at the right place at the right time.

Thelma Dunaitis for encouraging me from the very beginning and offering valuable suggestions.

Diana Wallis, an author and editor who was the first to tell me to rewrite the whole book. Thank you, Thelma, for getting us together.

Maria Sprafka, the editor who had to tell me to rewrite it again, but this time that I needed to take a lot out and put something else in. Thank you, Pam DiNardo, for getting us together.

Linda Robinson for coming into my life at the right time and for helping me whenever needed. You were a great encourager.

Susie Simpson for your ideas, suggestions, and prayer support.

Dee, Arbo, Gladys, my sisters-in-law, for helping with editing and formatting. Especially Dee, for the many hours of selfless, enthusiastic help when I needed it most.

Pastor Chuck and Gerry Hofmeister for reading my book and giving your blessing.

Ada Pollock for being my spiritual mother.

Mary Sue Eckard, Carolyn Putnam, Caroline Lawrence, Bev Wilson for saying the right thing at the right time, just right for my book.

For all my family and friends who have contributed and also encouraged me during these many years, thank you for your friendship, prayer, and support. I couldn't have done it without you.

Preface

Gentle Whispers

*After the earthquake came a fire, but the Lord was not
in the fire. And after the fire came a gentle whisper.*

1 KINGS 19:12

NOT KNOWING THAT I WAS in for a big encounter with
God, I was thinking this was going to be just another ordinary
writer's workshop. How many more conferences did I have to go
to before I would get a positive reply? Every time I would hear,
"Your book is definitely publishable, but you need to rewrite it."
How many more times would I have to hear that?

Wanting to get away from the hectic life and gear myself
for another rejection, I went to the main auditorium for a time
to relax. I sat alone, hoping to reprogram my negative mind
and praying that I would have a positive attitude going into the
workshop the next morning.

I knew I was to write this story and I knew it was my calling
because things—little, simple things—would appear, especially
when I was discouraged. One time, I just needed to get away
from it all, so my husband, Doyle, and I took a ride out on the

county roads. The beautiful autumn rays warmed my spirits as we soaked in the scenic views. We stopped at roadside apple orchards, garage sales, antique shops, and flea markets. It was at the flea market that I had my first gentle whisper from God.

Wandering and gazing at all the stuff for sale, I came upon a jewelry case. In it were earrings, pins, and necklaces made out of blue and white broken china. *Broken, useless dishes made into something beautiful.* I couldn't believe I was seeing this, and to this day I have not seen anything like it again. The color was even perfect. I bought a set of earrings and I treasure the meaning God gave me with His gentle whisper.

It was the surprising, unfailing, gentle whispers from God that gave me strength to keep writing when I felt completely unqualified and exhausted from life's trials, tests, and fires.

After each discouraging battle about writing, I would receive a surprising little gift, and it could be at any time. It would be slipped in the most unexpected place, and I would end up in a moment of gazing, in wonder and thought, almost in a daze. Could my God love me this much to take me out of the way to whisper a gentle encouragement?

For twenty-five years I struggled with each word and cried over each painful chapter, believing it was a lie that I could write a book, yet God kept telling me, "Naomi, keep going; never give up. *My power is made perfect in your weakness.*"

The marvels, the little gifts, the gentle whispers came in many more forms, each one with its own story, and they are carefully placed throughout my house as a reminder of God's faithfulness to me:

1. Fabric with blue and white broken dishes as the pattern.
2. Fabric with the words "Broken Dishes."
3. A card with a cracked china cup.
4. A calendar with a cracked china cup found in different patterns three different years (by Sandy Lynam Clough).
5. A real china cup with a crack painted on it with the words "God cares for you" (by Sandy Lynam Clough).
6. A little, framed picture of a cracked china cup with the words "Even in brokenness and sadness we find comfort in knowing there are those who care" (by Sandy Lynam Clough).
7. A quilt pattern called "Broken Dishes" given by a friend.
8. One Sunday I took my mom's Bible to church, and when I arrived a friend gave me material and notes that she took at a writing conference. That same morning in our Sunday school class they taught Mom's life verse.
9. Driving alone on a six-hour road trip, I had the radio on the whole way searching for stations, and each time they had an inspirational word just for me that I needed to hear.
10. A New England Village Series called, believe it or not, the Mullet Amish Farm.
11. I missed a Bible study and a friend told me I needed to listen to the video. In the middle of the night I woke up, watched it, and heard the words, "If you remain silent at this time . . . you and your father's family will perish. And who knows but that you have come to your royal position for such a time as this?" (Esther 4:14).
12. My sister Dorothy gave me a copy of a picture with a seagull trying to swallow a frog. The frog has his head in the seagull's mouth, but his hands are around the seagull's neck, trying to strangle him. The words written on the picture are "Don't *Ever* Give Up!"

Now you know why I knew I needed to write this book. I just couldn't stop—with each gentle whisper I would hear, "Naomi, keep going; never give up. *My power is made perfect in your weakness.*"

As at all conferences, everyone is upbeat, happy, and exuberant, wanting to spread the enthusiasm so you will catch the excitement and continue to pass it along. Me, I just wanted to know why this was such a struggle for me, to write this story about my mother, my parents. Would I ever catch the excitement to pass it along so that someone would see and want the same passion I have? I really wanted that excitement and delight in my soul. Now, all I knew was that I just needed to be obedient.

The music started and everyone was up, singing praises with joy. I joined in, but it hadn't reached my heart until all at once, after finishing a song, without a word the soloist started singing, "God is so good, God is so good, God is so good, He's so good to me." He stopped and said, "I don't know why I sang that song. It was not in the program and it was not planned. It must have been for someone here. You needed to hear the words 'God is so good.' I don't know why, but you needed to hear that."

My tears started when he was singing the song, then it was even harder to hold back the tears and running nose when he said, "I don't know why I sang that song. . . ."

Things look really ugly and embarrassing when you don't have a tissue to wipe your runny nose and mascara-filled tears. I was trying not to be noticed. Well, that didn't work, especially with strangers sitting right around me. I didn't want to get up, because now my eyes and nose were all red. Well, the tears and the running nose didn't stop, so off I went to the restroom.

The next morning we all gathered in the main auditorium before we went to the workshops. I went to the same area I had been the evening before and a group of people came up to me and asked if I was okay. They had seen what happened and knew the song was meant for me and just wondered why.

I said, "I came here for the writer's workshop because I am writing a book about my parents. In one of the chapters is a story about my mother when she was in a coma, and the first words from her were 'God is so good.' I struggle with writing and just wonder why I need to write this book, but every time I question it, God gives me a gentle whisper to encourage me to keep going, to never give up! Last night was a big one. God got my attention. I don't have to know why; I just have to be obedient."

After the assembly I went to purchase a CD of the soloist and looked at the list of songs. To my surprise, the song "I Must Tell Jesus" was on his CD, and you will later learn in this book why that was one more gentle whisper.

The interesting thing about this whole book is that when I started writing it in 1986, most of the story hadn't even happened. Things happened in 2005 that I wrote about. Now as I look back, I see that God taught me perseverance to keep going, to finish the task set before me, even though I was going through hard times. The astonishing thing about this is that God was always helping, encouraging me with His little gifts and gentle whispers.

We have an awesome God Who really loves us. Yes, really loves us! He wants all to come to Him, and He provided a way, through His precious Son, Jesus. He even encourages and helps us to be obedient even if it's hard . . . and after the fire comes a gentle whisper.

Why the Tears?

Those who sow with tears
will reap with songs of joy.
PSALM 126:5

THE THOUGHT OF GOING TO an Amish viewing darkened my spirit on this already dreary day. I didn't want to see relatives I didn't even know. My parents always made me go with them to visit their Amish relatives. My brother Fred was six years older and never had to go, so why did I? I didn't feel like changing my clothes and trudging out into the cold.

"Mom, can't I stay home? I'm eleven years old. I'm old enough to stay home by myself. Anyway, Fred's here. Can I stay? Please!" My mother ignored my questions as she instructed me to wear a plain dark dress. "I don't want to go. I don't even know your mom."

I knew that comment must have hurt Mom, but it was true.

"I really want you to. I want my family to meet you," Mother said as she placed her white head covering on her head. (Not like the

Amish prayer kapp with fancy pleats, just plain.) Taking a straight pin, she pinned the covering to her hair to keep it in place.

I'm glad I don't have to wear one of those, I thought. My older sisters used to have to wear them because they had been baptized. They didn't like it, but they had to wear them to church. Mom wore her covering all the time.

Every time we went to see our relatives, I had to wear plain dresses. Mom made all my dresses. Some were nice, pretty prints with lace, and some were plain with solid colors. When I went to school, all the girls had to wear dresses, so I didn't mind wearing them. After school, though, I would have loved to wear pants or shorts out to play, like all of my neighbors. That was not allowed, and I knew it. I overheard my mother and sisters having many arguments over the wearing of pants and shorts. I learned this rule when my sisters lived at home.

I dreaded the unpleasant thought of going with Mom and Dad to my grandma's viewing, but I knew I still had to. Being the youngest had some disadvantages, although I liked to visit my other Amish grandma. We would visit her almost every week, but for some reason we weren't welcome to visit my mother's parents.

We drove in a car to Middlefield, where my grandparents lived. As we approached the small, old, clay tile house (years ago it was a public school house), I saw the horses and buggies, but there was no car in sight. Starting to feel uncomfortable before even seeing one person, I said, "Why is it that we are the only ones here with a car? Aren't those buggies terribly cold in the winter?"

"Oh, they get used to it. They bundle up," Mom said.

"Well, I'm glad we don't have to ride in a horse and buggy. It would take forever to get somewhere. Why can't they have cars?" I asked.

"They are not allowed to have cars because of their religion," Mom replied.

"I have seen Amish in cars. How come they can ride in cars?" I asked.

"It is sort of confusing," Dad said. "They can ride in them, but they cannot own or drive them. Sometimes bishops allow them to own a vehicle if they need it for their occupation, but they are not allowed to drive it. They hire someone to drive it for them."

"What's the difference between driving a car and riding in a car? It doesn't make any sense," I said. "You are in a car no matter which one you are doing. If it's wrong to drive a car then it should be wrong to ride in a car. Driving or riding gets you to the same place. It doesn't make any sense to me. It's too confusing."

I might have had only one ride in a horse and buggy in all my growing up years. Can't say if I liked it or not, but I can say I am so glad we didn't have to ride in a horse and buggy, especially in the cold winter weather.

The conversation ended when Daddy pulled along the side of the road and we got out of the car. We walked to the house. Oh, how I dreaded this.

We entered the plain, dark, and dreary home lit only with dim lanterns. The smell of kerosene filled the rooms. People were sitting all around the room on benches. All the furnishings in the home had been removed. They were stored away and church benches were placed in rows in every room. The people wore very plain black and dark blue clothes. In the quiet, you could hear soft voices of people talking, and I wondered if they were whispering about us. We were not Amish and everyone else was. I felt like a defendant in a courtroom being analyzed by quiet jurors who would later deliberate my fate.

First we came to the kitchen. Everyone looked our way as we entered. It was full of men. As we made our way through the house, Daddy and Mom went around the rooms shaking hands. I wondered why we had to do this. Walking into this place was hard enough. Now shaking hands with each person seemed unbearable. I wanted to hide between my parents, but they would introduce me as though they were proud of me. I was beginning to believe that there was something about me that they wanted the Amish to see. A point to be made, something I knew nothing about. Why else would Mom want me to come along? She didn't make Fred come.

We came to another room where I saw Grandma's casket resting on two chairs. This room just had women in it, and we proceeded to shake hands with each of them. Mom would say, "Neomah [that is what she would call me], this is your aunt Fanny, my sister. This is your cousin Cora." The title *aunt* really didn't mean much to me. I never really knew what an aunt was, but when she said, "She's my sister," it made me think. *I have sisters and I see them all the time. How come Mom hardly ever sees her sisters?*

After what seemed like forever, we were finished shaking hands with each person there and walked over to where Grandma lay in a homemade pine-box casket. I looked at her but didn't recognize her and felt no sadness. She was a stranger to me. Mother stood and cried as Daddy wrapped his arms around us. As Mother wiped the tears away with her hankie, I wondered why she was crying. She never talked much about her mother. I don't ever remember her mother visiting us. I don't ever remember seeing letters or cards from her either. Not ever. So why was Mom so sad? I didn't know then what those tears really meant.

Daddy left us and went to sit with the men. Mom and I sat with the women. Mom talked to the ones around her as I leaned into her, seeking protection from all the strangeness around me.

One of the Amish women sitting by me asked, "Can you understand Dutch?" I think they asked because they didn't want to keep talking Dutch if I didn't understand.

"Yes, I can understand Dutch, but I can't speak it very well," I answered shyly. So they continued speaking Dutch. Daddy and Mom spoke a lot of Dutch in our home, but I never really talked it back to them. I would always answer in English. I wonder now how I knew the difference between Dutch and English.

I did not remember ever being in my grandparents' house before Grandma's funeral. All these people were my relatives, but I didn't know any of them. We never got together except for funerals, so I never learned to know these people.

The following day we went to the funeral. I don't remember much except for the dancing upstairs after the funeral and the meal. I was sort of surprised about the teens dancing because I was never allowed to dance, and here my Amish cousins were allowed. They even had a battery-operated radio, which I thought they were not allowed to have.

I was totally confused. Things they were not supposed to do, they did. Things I was not allowed to do, they were allowed, or were they? Maybe they did them even if they were not permitted, but dance at a funeral? Who would dance when they should be mourning? I really had no sorrow for Grandma because I never knew her, but they did. I felt so out of place in that upstairs room and I wanted out. Rescue came when someone said that they had placed the pie out for us to eat.

Even as a child, I knew I was different, very different! It felt like everyone was staring at me. I wondered what these Amish relatives were thinking. What did they think about me? Were they wishing they could be like me, or did they think I was bad and worldly? Why did my parents always want me to go with them to the Amish funerals? What did they think about my parents? What was their verdict? Why were we so different from all my other relatives?

How could I grow up in a home and never hear stories of what my family went through before I was born? Maybe they thought the past was best forgotten. Tucked away in my parents' minds were good memories and also memories of hard and sad times that we had never discussed. Did time heal those difficult moments in their lives? By the time I was old enough to be told such things, our conversations never led to those questions. Sometimes it takes a crisis to bring out those memories, which reveal the real meaning and beauty of a precious mother and father.

As the years passed, I began to find some of those tucked-away memories and treasures in my parents' lives. These stories demonstrated God's faithfulness in the lives of a simple, rebellious Amish man, his committed Amish wife, and the daughter born to them after they chose to leave that close-knit community. They are stories of life-changing choices, of heartbreak, and of joy. The stories proclaim the mighty truth that God continues to care for and work in the lives of the simple, the wounded, and the brokenhearted.

PART I

DADDY'S STORIES

Chapter 1

Unlike the Rest

. . . *"I praise you, Father, Lord of heaven and earth,
because you have hidden these things from the wise
and learned, and revealed them to little children."*

Matthew 11:25

THE MORNING HAD STARTED OUT all wrong. Simon's first frustration was with his older brothers, Owen and Elmer. All three slept in the same bed. The tugging of the blankets and the pushing and shoving annoyed Simon. Even worse was Owen's snoring. Simon would poke Owen with his elbow and he'd stop snoring for a while, but then he would start again, even louder than before. Simon was aggravated long before it was time to get up.

His brothers were out of bed with Dat's first wakeup call. By the time Simon got up, grumpy and still tired, Owen and Elmer had already gone downstairs, grabbed their jackets (they were all made alike) hanging on the coat hooks, and had gone out to the barn. It was the middle of November. The chilly morning fueled Simon's frustration even further, and now he couldn't find his jacket. He just wanted to get the chores done, return to the house, and crawl back into his warm bed. Where was his jacket?

"Owen probably took it," he mumbled under his breath. Disgusted, he kicked the shoes that were on the floor out of his way, found his boots, slipped them on, and headed for the barn.

Owen and Elmer were already milking the cows that Dat had prepped for milking before they got there.

"Simon, come on. Your job this morning is to clean out the manure." He heard a snicker coming from one of his brothers while his father, whom the children called Dat, was giving orders. "You are behind in your chores. You'll be late for breakfast and school. We need to get busy." Then he asked, "It's cool this morning; where is your jacket?"

"I couldn't find it," Simon said, mumbling.

"Well, you better find it. You don't want Mem to know you lost your jacket again. It will take her hours to sew you a new one. You boys grow out of them or ruin them fast enough. Now go to work, and when you're done try to find your jacket."

Simon heard Owen snickering again and it irritated him. *I'll get even*, he thought. *I'll sneak over when Dat isn't looking and show him a thing or two.*

Owen was sitting on a little three-legged stool, milking a cow. He had just turned his head the other way when Simon quietly sneaked up behind him. Simon kicked the stool out from under him and Owen fell off, bumping the bucket and spilling the milk.

Simon quickly ran back to work, acting like nothing happened.

Owen screamed out, "Dat, look what Simon did. He pushed me off the stool, spilling the milk all over."

Dat came running. "Simon, come over here."

Dat took Simon's arm and ordered a reply. Simon did not deny it, nor did he say he did it. Dat started to pull Simon toward the wall so he could get the leather strap hanging by the door for such an occasion as this. Simon was squirming to release himself. He knew all too well what he was going to get, and he wanted to loosen himself of his father's grip. He managed to free himself when Dat reached up to get the strap. He ran as fast as he could out of the barn and up to the house, hearing his father yell, "Wait until the chores are done and you're gonna get it!"

By the time he got up to the house, he thought, *Oh, no. If I go in, Mem will probably ask me why I'm in the house so early. She will ask if I finished my chores and send me right back out. Then she will holler at me and ask why I don't have on my jacket. I don't want to face that.*

Mem, Simon's mother, could be ornery, and she liked to tease at times. Maybe Simon got his mischievousness from her. She might even laugh at what he did. "I'll fix Dat and climb this tree and hide," he mumbled.

He climbed up the big maple tree that was right in front of the house. Underneath the tree was the water pump. A stone sidewalk led to the back door. The leaves were bright with an array of golden colors. The sky had a few tranquil, dark clouds that lined up along the horizon. The peaceful, dark-pink hues lightened in color as the sun slowly rose. Simon nestled on a limb, resting his back on the sturdy tree trunk and making sure he was out of sight. The chilly air made him wish for his jacket or, better yet, to be back in bed, but being chilly was better than a whipping.

He scanned his view from atop the tree, and it was beautiful. All around him he could see the large farm, with 160 acres full of sugar maple trees. Sugaring time was no fun. It was the one season he did not look forward to.

He noticed their old coonhound making his lazy way up the long lane from the road. Simon wondered what it had spent the night chasing. *Dumb old hound*, he thought, remembering the time Mem had sent him out with the table scraps to feed him. He had been lying by the back door.

"Come on, old hound," Simon had said. The dog knew he was going to get fed and waddled beside him, sniffing the whole way out to the barn. Simon picked up the dog bowl and placed it on top of the hay wagon then dumped the table scraps into the dog's bowl. There were still some mashed potatoes and gravy sticking on the bottom of the pan, so he got a corncob that was lying nearby and scraped the pan clean. He then placed the dog bowl on the ground, trying to avoid dumping it over as the anxious dog almost knocked it out of his hand. The old hound gobbled down the food. Simon squatted down as he watched him devour his meal. The hound didn't even care that his long ears were flopping in his food dish. He licked his chops, licked his bowl again, and then looked at the cob still in Simon's hand.

Simon looked at the hound staring at the cob and then looked at the corncob. He noticed it had some gravy and mashed potatoes still on it and decided to let the old hound lick off the cob. As he held the cob out to him, the old hound took hold of the cob, yanked it right out of his hand, and swallowed it. It got stuck in his neck and the old hound did some hard swallowing. He knew the dog was in serious trouble, but Simon did not know what to do. He could see the cob protruding in his neck. He started to get up, ready to run for help, when the old hound looked up, straightened out his neck, and swallowed one more time. Down the hatch it went.

Dumb old coonhound—all he's good for is a few good laughs, Simon thought, shaking his head.

The old hound was making his way by the barn when Owen and Elmer came out after finishing the chores. Elmer stooped down and patted the hound on the head. Owen ran ahead while Elmer encouraged the dog to follow him. Owen ran up the sidewalk and stopped at the water pump, right under the maple tree. He gave the long handle a few pumps, and out ran the water. He took the tin cup that was hanging on the pump and held it under the spout. The cold water filled the cup and ran over onto Owen's hands, getting the cuff of his jacket wet. He swung his arm to get the water off his hand and cuff while he drank the cup of cold water.

Elmer and the hound met Owen at the pump, and Elmer also got himself a drink. The old hound looked up the tree and barked one long, "Ah-woooof."

Simon saw Dat leave the barn and shut the door behind him. He was walking up to the house when the old hound barked. Simon cringed, knowing that dumb old hound was going to give away his hiding place if he didn't leave. The boys ran to the back door and into the house. The hound lay down by the tree, making a grunting sound as he stretched out. He rolled over on his back then moved back and forth, scratching himself.

"What did you find last night, old boy? I heard you barking," Dat said as he stooped and scratched the hound's belly. "You're a good old coon dog."

Simon could not believe Dat liked that hound, but for some reason he did. Dat stood up, turned around, looked right up the tree, and said, "Simon, breakfast is ready. Get yourself down here. I'll be waiting for you."

Ach. Why didn't I stay and take it? Simon thought. *Thinking about getting a whippin' is always worse than the whippin' itself.* He did get the whipping and he wasn't ever going to try that stunt again.

The looks and chuckles from his brothers and sisters as he walked into the kitchen after the whipping were even worse. He walked over to the sink and started to pump the short handle.

"Hurry up, Simon," his mother said. Simon washed his hands, wiped them on a towel, and took his place at the table. They all bowed their heads in silent prayer. He squinted as he peeked out to see when Dat lifted his head from prayer. He wondered what Dat was praying silently.

Breakfast was not as good as usual, maybe because of the snickering.

"Come on, boys, stop it and get ready for school. The wagon will be here to pick you up soon enough," Mem said as she lifted Joe out of the highchair and placed him on the floor. Emma, their younger sister, handed baby Mary Ann to Mem and was ready to rush out ahead of the boys.

"Simon, look for your jacket at school today. You probably left it there," Mem said as she waved goodbye and closed the door.

When Simon arrived at school he didn't find his jacket in his room. His teacher sent Simon to the superintendent's office in case it was left outside and taken to the Lost and Found. He did not want to go. The office was just a little room, but going there seemed like a big, scary task. The superintendent was a large man who gave whippings if the teacher couldn't make a boy or girl listen. Even though Simon was just looking for his jacket, he was frightened. He had never gotten a whipping from the superintendent, but he had had his fingers whacked with a ruler by teachers a few times throughout his school years for misbehaving. Boy, did it sting.

This was a public school. He learned to speak English there, but at home they spoke Pennsylvania Dutch. Like the other Amish students, he would only finish the eighth grade and then work at home with the family. There were no Amish schools at the time.

"Simon, I found your jacket," Owen said on the wagon ride home from school.

"Found it? You didn't find it. You forgot yours yesterday and took mine this morning," Simon said accusingly. Grabbing the jacket away from Owen, he sat down beside his buddy Jake.

"I can't wait to get home. I heard Dat say at breakfast that Uncle Will might stop by today," Simon began excitedly. "He's hauling Amish up from Plain City for a visit. When he does, he stops by and sees us sometimes. He has a car and I'm gonna sit in the driver's seat right when I get home," Simon explained. "Every time he comes, I get in his car and turn the wheel, play with the buttons, and pretend to shift. He ain't Amish. I wish I wasn't Amish. Someday I will have an automobile. I don't care if we're allowed to or not. I'm havin' one!"

Simon was the first to jump off the wagon when it got close to their home. The horses had not even come to a complete stop before he was off and running down the long lane. He flung his jacket and lunchbox on the grass and ran to the car. He took hold of the door handle and pulled. It didn't open. He ran around and tried all the other doors but they were all locked.

Dat and Uncle Will were standing by the barn laughing.

"I told Uncle Will he better lock his car or you'd sneak in it when you came home," Dat called out, laughing with a twinkle in his eye.

Simon knew all too well that his family was different from Uncle Will, and he did not like it. He later asked his father, "Why can Uncle Will have an automobile and we can't?"

"Wir sin Amish [We are Amish]," Dat said.

"Well, it just doesn't make sense. When I get big I'm going to get an automobile," Simon said firmly.

CHAPTER 2

Mischievous Behavior

*Jesus said, "Let the little children come to me, and do
not hinder them, for the kingdom of heaven belongs to
such as these."*

MATTHEW 19:14

MESOPOTAMIA IS A SMALL, QUIET town nestled in north-eastern Ohio, sometimes referred to as Mespo. In the middle of town is a road circling a park of big, beautiful sugar maple trees which, during the winter at sugaring time, would have lots of sap buckets hanging on them. On the south end of the circle is a hitching post for the horses and buggies. Across the road, on the southwest side of the circle, is a country store with large white pillars that go up to the second floor, and to the west of the store is the school.

This snowbelt area, caused by the lakefront effects from Lake Erie, was a child's winter-wonderland playground full of laughter, thrills, and chills. Route 87 was the main road that went in front of the school in Mesopotamia where the children attended. West of the school was a long road that descended like a ski slope. It was covered with layers of ice and snow, perfect for sledding.

Walking up the huge slope took quite a while, but the hike was worth it. The road wasn't traveled much because there weren't many cars, and horses and buggies didn't travel it often because of the ice and snow, making it perfect for clear sledding.

Taking one sled, Jake, Owen, and Simon climbed on, lying on top of each other three-high. They made certain they were secure by holding on to the sled and lying still. Elmer and his buddy Dan took the other sled and positioned themselves far enough away but beside them, like starting to gear up for a race.

"Get ready. Get set. Go!" Off they went, gliding down the slope with the wind and snow blowing in their faces. They had thrills in their tummies that made chills run through their whole body. Finally leveling off, they coasted to a stop.

"We made it without falling off!" The boys proclaimed, excited about the ride.

"Let's do it again," Elmer said.

"Ah, I want to, but I don't want to hike up the big hill again," whined Dan.

"What if we get a horse to pull us back up the hill?" Simon suggested.

"Let's do it again, but you know we can't get a horse," Elmer replied.

"Come on, let's go!" coaxed Jake.

Off they went trudging up the big hill for the second time. Who knows—they might do it for the third time just for the thrill.

The road in front of their farm had smaller hills than the long one at the school, but it was still fun, and they didn't have to hike so far to get to the top. The boys would place lanterns on fence posts or trees and sled ride all evening long. Yes, winter was fun except for when sugaring time came.

Winter in Geauga County is known for its maple sugaring. (Actually Mesopotamia was in the Northwest corner of Trumbull County bordering Geauga County; mistakenly most people would include Mespo in Geauga County.) It was the time Simon didn't like because of all the long, hard hours, but it was a family affair and everyone had to do their part. The farm had a grove of sugar maple trees called a sugar bush. To prepare for making syrup, they located, identified, and tapped the maple sugar trees. To tap them, they used a hand drill and drilled a hole, hammering in the spout with a hook called a spile. Then they hung all the sap buckets on the spiles.

Workhorses pulled the sled as the boys poured the sap from the buckets into the gathering tank once a day taking the sap to the sugar house. There they boiled the sap into pure maple syrup, which took all day and seemed like forever. Sometimes they would be out in the sugar house until two o'clock or so in the morning. They had to watch, being careful to get the syrup up to the right temperature and keeping it there by tending to the wood fire.

The fragrance of sweet maple filled the sugar house. The steam and smell from the bubbling liquid lingered on their clothes and ascended throughout the surrounding fields as it combined with the scent of burning wood. When the syrup was at a perfect consistency, they would fill half-gallon glass jars with the delicious syrup. Then they would start the boiling process all over again with a new batch of sap the next day.

They had to do this with all the maple trees on this 160-acre farm. Dat must have thought that he didn't have enough trees, so he rented the maple trees from the farm next to him also. What a job! No time for playing or sledding; they were busy every minute.

One evening Simon was put in charge of taking the syrup to the house. He had a bright idea: If he put the twelve jars in a wheelbarrow he wouldn't have to make so many trips to the house. The wheelbarrow was wooden and flat, with a headboard in the front. He filled the wheelbarrow up and had his younger brothers protect it while he went back to the sugar house to close the door. But, wouldn't you know it, the younger brothers were not watching close enough and their younger sister sat on the edge of the wheelbarrow. Down fell Alma, the wheelbarrow landed on its side, and the twelve half-gallon glass jars came crashing down, spilling all the sweet liquid gold on the dirty snow. All those hours of hard labor were gone. All that was left was one sticky mess. Simon didn't want his younger sister to get in trouble, so he took all the blame. Even worse, he felt bad for the great loss of income for the family. Simon was good at getting himself in sticky messes, one right after the other. Following this incident, he always dreaded maple sugaring. When the trees started to bud, sugaring season was over.

One day, Dat brought home a big box of junk from an auction. The boys loved to make things with old junk. Once when

Dat wasn't around, Simon sneaked into the shop and looked through the box of junk. He found a fifty-caliber bullet about five inches long. It was probably a World War I bullet. Simon was curious and wanted to see if it was any good. So he put the bullet in a vise to hold it, took a hammer, and gave the primer a good whack. That fired the bullet off with a loud *blast*. The bullet took off through the tool shed door, into one corner of the barn, and out the other corner of the barn and went whistling off into the deep woods.

Another time Simon was fooling around with a gun and had another bright idea and wanted to test it out. He put a ball bearing down the barrel in front of the bullet. Not being sure what would happen if he pulled the trigger, he got his partner in crime, Joe, to do the test.

"Hey, Joe, go take this gun outside and shoot it," Simon said, knowing full well he was using his younger brother for an experiment. Joe was six years younger and did whatever his older brother asked.

Joe took the gun outside and pulled the trigger. It exploded! It was not like a regular gunshot; it was an explosion because the ball bearing kept the bullet from escaping the barrel. When Simon looked at Joe and saw all the blood on his face, he thought that he had blown out his brother's eye. Joe got a gash above his eye and messed up his forehead for quite a while, leaving a scar. Thank goodness that was all that happened. Simon could have been in big trouble in both of those bullet incidences.

Another time, Uncle Harv was visiting from Plain City, Ohio. He was six years older than Dat and had never married.

He rode a Harley Davidson motorcycle and owned a business selling them.

Off to the side of the barn was parked this nice, big, shiny motorcycle. Simon's eyes popped open when he saw it and right away he wanted to investigate. He knew he shouldn't, but he just couldn't help himself. When it came to modern machinery, automobiles, motors, motorcycles, and the like, Simon was curious. He just wanted to take a closer look, that's all.

It had wonderful gadgets. This was better than a car. You didn't have to open the hood to see the motor. Oh, this thing was great. He walked around a few times, looking intently. He felt the leather seat and wondered how it felt to sit on the seat and hold on to the handlebars. *Oh, what fun it must be to drive fast. It might feel like sledding down Mespo hill on Route 87 with the wind blowing in my face,* he thought.

He couldn't resist. He carefully climbed onto the tilted cycle and sat on the seat, grabbing hold of the handlebars. He imagined what it would be like riding.

"Simon, you better get off. Dat's coming!" Joe quietly called as he anxiously waited for his brother's safety. Simon climbed off, but he lost his balance. Down went Simon and down went the motorcycle. Once again, Simon was in trouble! Simon may never have gotten a whipping from the feared school superintendent, but he got plenty from Dat!

CHAPTER 3
Adventurous Years

Do not turn to the right or the left;
keep your foot from evil.

PROVERBS 4:27

IT WAS EARLY FALL BUT chilly enough for a fire to be started in the black potbelly stove in the living room. The older boys had finished with farming chores and were coming in to warm up around the stove and settle in for the evening. The older girls were helping Mem put the younger children in bed, except Emma.

Emma was working diligently on her organdy kapp, the Amish prayer cap. It was tedious work and took many hours to iron in all the small pleats on the back of the kapp.

Mem had finally joined them and sat by the potbelly stove in a small rocking chair with a big bowl of apples in her lap. She took a knife and started to peel the apples, placing the sliced apples in another bowl. Once in a while one of the children would snatch the peeled apples. She didn't mind, except when she felt that she was not going to have enough for the schnitz pies she wanted to make.

The boys had tired with reading and one would doze off to sleep. They were at a singing the night before and were out late with their girls so they were sleepy. Mem finished peeling her apples and took the bowls out into the kitchen.

Mem had an ornery streak in her and always found someone to tease. She would take peanut butter, mustard, or jelly and place it on the sleeping boy's nose, and when the boy would rub his nose he would smear it all over. Mem would laugh and laugh. Owen, the oldest boy, would get really frustrated at Mem sometimes, but he would never hit her, though he came close. So to stay clear of her young strong boys, she would get someone else, even one of the boys if they were awake, to do the dirty work.

Simon dozed off, and he got mustard put on his finger. They took a feather and tickled his nose. He rubbed his nose and got mustard smeared all over his face. He jumped up, accusing Emma of doing it, but no one confessed. Even so, there still was a lot of laughter.

Emma tried to look innocent even with her snickering and kept working with her kapp. She was done with the pleating and had sewn in the final stitches. All she needed to do was the final pressing of the band and ribbon. She held up her kapp, examining it carefully, pleased with her work.

It was a similar evening when Dat came home and announced, "Look what I got from Bill. A phonograph!"

"John, you are not going to bring that in for these boys. You know what that leads to!" Mem said, disgusted.

"Well, they need to listen to something," Dat said, ignoring Mem. "Here, boys, help me with this and get this phonograph to work."

They moved it in and wound up the phonograph. They slipped round records into a big disk and enjoyed the music.

"Bill told me to take the phonograph, keep the records, give them to the boys, and let them play them as long as they want to," Dat said, trying to convince Mem that it was all right to listen to records.

"Wild Bill?" Mem said, mumbling as she left the room. "You know what he is!"

Wild Bill was a neighbor who lived at the corner of the road they lived on. Charlie, also a neighbor, lived right beside Wild Bill. Charlie went for the cows one morning and he saw somebody lying in the grass in the middle of a field. Charlie walked up to him and said, "Bill, what's wrong?"

"Oh, I was sleeping," Bill stammered.

Still not satisfied with his answer, Charlie said, "What's wrong? Don't you feel good? Why are you lying down like this in the middle of a field, so early in the morning?"

"No, last night the ground flew up and hit me in the head," Bill said, as serious as could be.

Everybody knew Mem didn't want the phonograph in the house and that it would probably soon disappear. It was just like the piano that was in the house when Dat bought the farm. Dat played the piano and was good at it. The Amish neighbors heard the music in the summer when the windows were open and told the bishops. The bishops made a visit and told Dat to move the piano out. So he did—out onto the porch. Well, the bishops made another visit, then Dat had to move it out into the barn, but he never got rid of it.

It was the same way when they first moved up to Geauga County. Dat had a car, and when the Amish neighbors saw him drive it, they reported it to the bishops.

One day Emma was outside raking and working in the yard. Simon, out of sheer orneriness, appeared out of nowhere and snatched Emma's kapp right off her head. As he was running away from her, he wrinkled her kapp in his hands. Emma, screaming, ran after him. Simon threw the wrinkled kapp at her. At a quick glance, Emma knew the hard work she had put into making the kapp was destroyed, and anger erupted. She was determined to get him back. She ran after him with the rake, which was a perfect weapon. The first chance she had, she flung the rake with the long teeth at him. The rake caught him and the teeth sank into his arm.

The boys were mischievous, but they did have 160 acres to be mischievous on. They would find all sorts of Indian artifacts, tomahawks, arrowheads, and knives, saving them in boxes and storing them away in safe keeping. Rumor has it that there is still a box missing and that it might be in what was the old washhouse, hidden up in the eaves.

On their many searching and hunting adventures, they also found snakes. Lots and lots of big black snakes, way over a hundred—too many to count—in what you might call a snake pit. There were ravines and gullies on their property with big, beautiful cliffs that looked like box canyons. There was a creek running through their land, and the creek bed was lined with all flat stones. The snakes had many places to hide in the big woods, but they would sometimes find themselves close to the farm. Once there was a snake that slithered up the side of the house and was sunning itself on the upstairs window ledge. The window was open and there was a baby sleeping in her bed, right by the window. Needless to say, they killed many snakes on that farm.

The boys learned how to walk on stilts and got pretty good. They also made their own stilts all different heights. Stealing Dat's harnesses, they would cut them up and use the leather for straps. They used the straps on the top of the one-by-four to hold on to, and they would use straps to secure their feet. Dat would get so mad when a harness came up missing. Sometimes the boys hid under the workbench to hide from Dat if they were making something they should not have been. Some stilts were so high that they could even touch the eave spouts and some were so great that they couldn't even get into the barn door upstairs—that big, high, barn door. They would climb on top of the barn roof or other buildings to get started. But, boy, when they fell, that was a tough one and they felt it. For other heights, to get started they crawled onto the hay mound in the barn and bowed way down to get out of the barn door. The small stilts were about seven to eight feet tall. They used the small stilts to have races and see how fast they could outrun each other.

There was a bounty on crows and red-tailed hawks because they were destroying crops. The birds were a real nuisance for the farmers. So, for every bird leg someone took to the county seat, they got a shotgun shell. Simon had this great idea. He got his little brother Joe to go with him in the big woods. They would shimmy up huge, tall trees and steal the young out of the nests. That way he didn't waste any shotgun shells to get these birds.

Their neighbor Charlie had a fruit orchard. The boys would sneak over at night and eat grapes and peaches, or whatever fruit was in season. Charlie would hear or see them and call out, "Are you boys out there again?"

When the boys heard him coming, they took off through the field as fast as they could, trying never to get caught and hoping that Charlie would never tell Dat that the boys stole his fruit.

Amish teenagers can pretty much do what they want. There is really no discipline from the church for them. But when they join the Amish church, it's a different story. Most Amish parents let their teenagers get out their wild streak and act like they don't notice what their children are doing and say, "When they get married, they will settle down." This is what the Amish call Rumspringa, running-around years.

Simon and his brothers would go to the country store in Mespo and listen to the fights that were broadcasted on the radio. There was a lot of static, and it was hard to hear, but it still was entertainment. Stealing was one thing they were taught not to do, but Simon somehow just couldn't help himself. When they went to the country store in Mespo, Simon would slip things into his pocket. He never did get caught, or so he thought.

CHAPTER 4

TWO VOWS

But for you who revere my name, the sun of righteous-
ness will rise with healing in its wings. And you will
go out and leap like calves released from the stall.

MALACHI 4:2

SIMON'S REBELLIOUS SPIRIT WAS BURIED deep inside
him. He grew up being the ornery one in the family who teased
a lot, which sometimes got him into trouble. He tolerated the
religion and went along with all their ways to keep peace because
he loved his family. He had many questions about their religion
because, to him, some things just didn't make sense. Why could
some people have telephones, radios, pianos, and phonographs, and
they couldn't? Why did Mem have to sew all their clothes and
others could buy theirs? What about tractors and cars? Yes, cars?
Why have those rickety, slow horse and buggies when you can
have a nice, fast car? It just didn't make sense. Soon he would get
married and get away from living under his mother and father's
roof and do what he wanted.

Simon really liked working on the big, beautiful farm. He worked on the farm with his father and six brothers and five sisters until he was twenty-two years old. He had met a young, beautiful girl at an Amish singing some years back whose name was Susan. An Amish singing is held on Sunday nights at a home where the young folks gather and sing songs and hymns. From there, some may pair off and go out for the night. The boy would drive the girl home in his horse and buggy, and she would ask him in.

Susan had said her vows, promising to obey the Ordnung (Amish church ordinances—man-made rules) and was baptized a member of the Old Order Amish church, the strictest sect of the Amish. She came from a very large family who lived in Middlefield, Ohio, the center of the Amish community. She was beautiful with black hair and dark eyes to match. They wanted to get married, but Simon had to be baptized and become a member of the Amish church first before he was permitted to marry Susan. Simon didn't realize the seriousness of the vows he was taking the day he was baptized.

Simon and Susan were published, which means an Amish deacon is chosen by the bridegroom to be the one to ask the bride's parents for his permission to marry their daughter. At the next church service, the deacon announces, or publishes, the wedding date. Simon and Susan said their wedding vows on March 17, 1938, with a big Amish wedding service. Susan wore a new blue dress and Simon a new dark navy blue suit, all home-sewn. Amish weddings are usually held on weekdays, and theirs was on a Thursday.

Their first home was on a farm which Simon called the Radke Farm in Claridon and they were the hired hands. Claridon was just northwest of Middlefield, a small town with a little country store and a church on the crossing of the main roads. They lived on the Radke Farm for two years, just a little southeast of the main intersection. Their first son, Atlee, was born in that farmhouse on April 3, 1939.

Pete was Simon's young horse who hadn't been let out in the pasture all winter. When they took him out of his stall to hitch him to the buggy, he sometimes got a little out of hand. One day Susan wanted to visit her parents, so Simon went out and hitched Pete to the buggy. Pete actually stood still and behaved himself while Simon was getting him ready. Simon then helped Susan and the baby get into the buggy.

"Now, be careful. Pete sometimes can be ornery," Simon instructed as Susan took hold of the lines. Simon knew how dumb that horse used to act. When Simon was single he would drive that wild horse real hard, hoping to break it in. While in training, Pete would stand on his hind legs with his front legs way up in the air. He'd come down onto the buggy shaft with his head right where his behind should have been. One time while they were trying to hitch him up to the buggy, Pete lay down and wouldn't get up, so Dat said to Simon, "Get on the buggy. I'll get him up." He took a handful of sand and held Pete's ear up then let the sand run in Pete's ear. Pete immediately shot up like a bullet, shaking his head. Horses aren't any good unless they are broken in. Now Simon thought Pete was finally broken in.

"Oh, I can handle him," Susan said. She was a strong woman with determination and was not afraid of trying things. She had grown up with horses, and she was used to driving them. She took the lines and they were off.

Pete took off out the lane and across the road like a streak of lightning and into the neighbor's horseshoe-shaped driveway. They went around the curve and back out. Susan turned him and got him back in the lane where Simon was running toward her. She got Pete to stop. Simon helped Susan and the baby out of the buggy.

"Susan, you go back in the house for a while. I am going to take care of Pete," Simon said.

Simon got in the buggy and took Pete for a ride down the road. Simon opened Pete up and let him run. He ran like he was a racehorse free from the stall that confined him. He let Pete run as long as he wanted. Pete knew who was behind the reins then. After Pete started to slow down, Simon took him back home.

Simon told Susan, "Get in the buggy. Now you can drive him." She drove Pete down through Burton, all the way through Middlefield to her parents' home without any trouble. She stayed all day. On the way home Pete was a little ornery starting off, but her father helped get Pete ready. He was fine the rest of the way home for her.

One Sunday when they came home from church, Mr. Radke had been working on the farm. He said to Simon, "We just put up an electric fence in the pasture. You can leave the cows out tomorrow in the hayfield." Simon had just taken the first cutting of hay from that field a few days before.

Simon said, "Okay," and trusted him. So he never bothered to check the wire. Mr. Radke had hooked it up with live wire without any relay in it and put the hot wire right through it. The next day Simon put out the cows and horses in the hayfield. He was out in the field when he saw Pete reach over the fence to get a bite of corn that had just been cut off. Pete's chest touched the electric fence; the shock knocked him down and killed him instantly. Mr. Radke gave Simon seventy-five dollars to go buy another horse. He went and bought Pete's sister.

Simon and Susan were happy living and working on the farm even with some sad times. The farm was more work than just one man could handle, so Susan helped out as much as she could. She had the house to keep clean, along with cooking, gardening, canning, sewing, and caring for a little baby.

In the spring, Simon needed to plant the crops and would be in the fields late at night working. He would stop just long enough to get the cows in from the field and feed them. Then he would go back into the fields. Susan would milk all twenty-five cows by herself twice a day. They had a single-unit milk machine, but after using that, she had to follow up by stripping all the cows. *Stripping* is making sure all the milk is out. If you don't get all the milk out, they can get mastitis, an inflammation of the udder, and then the milk is no good.

Susan worked too hard and lost her second baby in her sixth month. Simon got Dr. Reed, and he came to the farmhouse. He helped Susan, but he couldn't save the baby. Susan was heartbroken, but there was nothing that could be done.

Dr. Reed wrapped him up in a blanket and handed the baby boy to Simon.

Simon said, "What shall I do with him?"

"Well." He paused. "Find a favorite place on the farm that Susan liked, make a box and put him in, and bury him," the doctor said sadly.

So Simon let Susan hold the baby until he made the box and dug the grave. He buried their second son at the end of the clothesline, where Susan had planted some flowers.

Simon didn't like that Susan had to work so hard, so he bought his own clothes and as a result, she had one less job. He had Susan take off the shirt pockets because they were not allowed to have them. One day Simon had been shopping in Middlefield when an Amish preacher stopped him. The preacher said, "Simon, what kind of light are you to the world?"

Simon said, "Why do you ask?"

"I see you have a store-bought shirt on," the preacher said. "You know you're not allowed to wear them. You're only allowed to wear homemade clothes your wife has sewn for you!"

"How do you know it's a store-bought shirt?" Simon questioned. "It has no pocket."

"Oh, yes, I can tell. I know it's store-bought. I can tell it's not home-sewn, and neither are your pants," the preacher accused.

The next time Simon went to church, the bishop made him kneel in front of all the people and confess. Confess that he had failed God and the Amish church for wearing store-bought clothes. Simon said it, but he didn't mean it. He confessed so he could keep peace because he had broken a rule. In his heart, he didn't care and didn't want to keep the Amish rules and traditions.

Simon knew from that moment on, things would never be the same. He began to feel like a pent-up horse kept in a stall all winter.

CHAPTER 5

Amish Rebel

Do not remember the sins of my youth and my rebellious ways; according to your love remember me, for you, Lord, are good.

PSALM 25:7

"SIMON, I WISH YOU WOULDN'T play that radio in the house when the children are around to hear. You know what the bishops would say if they saw you right now!" Susan exclaimed as she cleared the dishes from the table. She became frustrated. The children were noisily playing on the floor, getting in her way as she walked to the kitchen sink. "Simon, I mean it! You know you shouldn't have those two vehicles in the driveway either. You're going to get caught someday!"

"Oh, those bishops don't bother me," Simon said as he got up from the kitchen table and made his way to the door.

"I'll be right back in." Simon went out to have his cigarette. Susan didn't want him to smoke in the house, so he would go outside to smoke his pipe or cigarettes. While he was out there, he checked the milk truck to make sure it was ready for the next day.

Simon wanted to get away from the Amish community, so he had gotten a job driving a milk truck for a dairy in Painesville about twenty-five miles north of Middlefield. Another bonus for driving the milk truck was that it was the closest he could get to driving a vehicle without owning his own. The bishop's rules didn't permit him to have a license and to drive, but that didn't stop him. The family also rented a house with electricity, and he drove a station wagon that his boss let him have to drive for his family.

Simon finished his cigarette and then went back into the house. He then went to the icebox and pulled out a bottle of beer. Susan was washing dishes. He went close to her and kissed her on the neck. *She's beautiful. She works hard—sometimes too hard. Hope she doesn't lose this one*, he thought, sadly reflecting on when she lost their baby boy.

Simon grew sad for her as he thought about the baby, still placing small kisses on her neck. "Simon, stop that!" Susan snapped, pulling her neck away to escape his kisses.

Her comment startled his reflecting, and he wished he could escape what he knew was coming.

"I mean it! You know we made a promise when we were baptized that we would obey the Ordnung!" Susan had not finished the conversation when he had gone out to have his cigarette, so she brought up the subject again.

"Oh, those rules—they mean nothing to me. I'll do what I want to!" He went to the icebox again and this time took out a six-pack. He placed the unopened bottle back in the pack. "Hey, where is the bottle opener?" he said, trying to change the subject.

"Simon, you know you shouldn't be drinking that stuff."

Simon didn't seem to care what she was saying as he took the six-pack with the bottle opener and walked away into the living room.

What a sight, Susan thought as she peeked around the corner to check on the children. Their father was slouching in a chair, a bottle of beer in his hand with the remaining six-pack sitting on the floor. The radio blared out with that evil hillbilly music.

"Simon," she said in a loud voice. "Turn that evil thing down. Better yet, get rid of it."

Simon pretended not to hear and let the music play. Susan was getting angry, but what could she do? She loved that ornery man. It wasn't unusual for the young Amish boys to do wild things before they were married, during Rumspringa. Parents are usually happy when their sons get married because it settles them down a little when they start having families. When she was dating Simon, she knew he had different ideas, but she thought that, like all the rest, he would settle down once they were married.

He had not settled down. In fact, he was getting worse. Having three children and one on the way didn't seem to change his wild ideas at all. Susan knew if he wouldn't change his ways, the bishops would soon be after him again, no matter how far away they lived.

She walked out to the kitchen table to finish cleaning up the dishes when she noticed a horse and buggy coming down the road. *Strange*, she thought. *A horse and buggy in this neck of the woods. Who could that be? Could it be family? No, it's too late in the afternoon for them. It is too long a ride to stay just a little while. The bishops or dea-*

cons? No! Not tonight! Simon will be shunned [meidung] for sure if they see him now! Her heart pounded; her anger surged. *Why did Simon have to be this way? Why couldn't he just obey the rules?*

As the horse and buggy turned into the driveway, she tucked her loose hair into her Amish prayer kapp, straightened her apron around her pregnant belly, and went to tell Simon someone was there. But before she went, she took one last peek to see if she knew who the visitors were. Sure enough, it was just what she had feared. *The bishops!* Blood rose in her neck. Her heart raced. What should she do? Would she have enough time to warn Simon so that he could get rid of the radio and change his clothes? It was too late. The car and the milk truck in the driveway were the thing they were probably coming to talk to him about. No, she didn't have enough time to warn him. She knew he was caught. Anyway, they probably heard the music. It seemed loud enough to go through the walls. *Well, maybe if the bishops catch Simon, it will teach him a lesson,* she thought. *I'm mad enough to let them in without even telling him that they are here.*

Before she knew it, the bishops were knocking on the kitchen door. She thought for sure that Simon heard it, but the music was so loud, he never heard them enter the house.

"Ve bish du [How are you]?" the bishops said as they entered the kitchen, taking off their big black hats.

"I'm fine," Susan replied.

"We're here to see Simon," the bishops demanded.

"He's in the living room." She pointed toward the room, gathering the children toward her to get them out of the bishops' way.

As her anger subsided, a sickening feeling crept into the pit of her stomach. *What have I done? Why can't things be different?*

Simon was awakened with a start. "Simon, why don't you throw that radio out the window?" the bishops thundered.

Simon sat up, looked at the bishops, and then glared at Susan. He placed the empty bottle of beer on the floor and turned off the radio. Before he could give them a greeting, they were preaching to him about the rules.

He knew well enough about the rules, and he hated them. He would never forget the incident of the preacher confronting him about his store-bought clothes.

The night those two bishops entered the music-filled room, Simon was wearing a store-bought shirt and store-bought bib overalls. Parked in the driveway were a milk truck and his boss's station wagon. In his wallet was his chauffeur's license. They had caught him.

He had no intention of going in front of the church and confessing again. He knew those rules and traditions didn't change his heart. But he wasn't going to let the bishops know that. He let the bishops say what they needed to say and then saw them to the door.

"Well, that was a surprise. Wasn't it?" Susan snickered.

"Yeah, why didn't you tell me they were here?" Simon said as he started to walk back into the living room.

"You never listen to me, so I thought you'd learn the hard way," she said, hoping that the bishops had finally gotten through to him.

"Well, that didn't learn me anything. I'm paying no attention to what those Amish bishops said to me. They didn't say anything about the beer I was drinking because they are both alcoholics. Yes, those Amish bishops!" he mocked. "They came here to tell me how wrong I am living. Those Amish bishops said, 'Why don't you open the window and throw the radio out?' They didn't tell me to throw the beer out because they like it too well themselves. In fact, I'm so sick of those bishops, I may enlist in the army!" he concluded with a rebellious tone.

Susan's voice rose. "Oh, Simon, you wouldn't! You made a vow before God and the church to obey the rules." (The Ordnung forbids anything to do with war or politics.)

"I might have made that promise, but I didn't mean it. I really didn't know what it all meant. I had to get baptized and make that promise in order to marry you!"

Simon walked into the living room, took another bottle of beer, opened it, slouched into the chair, and took a drink. "I have been seeing some soldiers while I'm delivering milk in town. I like how they look in their uniforms. I want to get away from all these Amish rules and see what the world is like. I never wanted to be Amish. Even as a little boy, I wondered what it was like to not be Amish and have cars. I always told my dad I would have a car someday!"

"Simon, you know you wouldn't leave me and enlist in the army. You have three children and I am about to have a baby any time. You can't leave me. You can't go! A war is going on. It's against the rules." Susan pleaded with him, but she knew that someday he would leave the church. In a way, he already had left the church. But leave her? She never believed he would leave her. Her heart ached at the thought.

That dreadful day came for Susan when Simon did enlist in the army on September 13, 1944, during World War II. Her heart was broken, and her life was shattered. Susan had their fourth child, Betty, September 28, and Simon left for active duty on December 14, 1944. She was left alone with four small children ages five, three, two, and two months. She was deserted in a town away from family. Simon was a disgrace to the Amish community. Her husband was destined to be shunned, and she was married to him. She wanted so much to keep the Amish rules. She had made a promise-vow to God and the church, but she had also made a promise-vow to stay married to Simon.

Her family came up to Painesville, packed up all her belongings, and moved Susan and the children back to Middlefield, back home in the Amish community. There they took care of her. She received checks from the army while Simon was serving, but the bishops wouldn't let her use the money. Susan deposited the money in a savings account. Her family wanted her to leave Simon and have nothing to do with him. She was confused, angry, and hurt.

Simon was proud to be in the army, and he loved his army uniform. He didn't look different and strange. He looked just like any other American in uniform. No one knew of his different religion with all the restrictions about clothes. He felt normal. It felt nice, but yet there was still an empty feeling inside, like something wasn't right. He had had that feeling before, but he had always thought it was because of the Amish. Simon was searching for something more to life than rules and traditions. He knew just obeying those rules did not give him peace. He went to talk to the chaplain about his feeling and told him all about his background.

The chaplain said, "Simon, it's not the kind of clothes you wear that will fill that empty feeling you have. You have that empty feeling because you need Jesus."

The chaplain tried to explain some things in the Bible, but it was too confusing. Simon couldn't understand. He never really could understand the things the bishops preached about either. Nothing made sense.

CHAPTER 6

The Homecoming

The Lord is close to the brokenhearted
and saves those who are crushed in spirit.

PSALM 34:18

SIMON RECEIVED AN HONORABLE DISCHARGE on August 10, 1945, and he made plans to go home to Susan and his four children. Surely things would be different now. Susan would know that he was serious about leaving the Amish religion, and surely she would stop pressuring him to obey the rules. He was sure that joining the army and leaving her had taught Susan a big lesson.

Simon arrived in Middlefield, where Susan and the children were living with Susan's sister. He got out of the car, took out his duffel bag, swung the strap over his shoulder, and walked up to the front door. Simon looked good in his army clothes and walked proudly that day, excited about seeing his family.

The front door swung open and he saw Susan. On his way home he had imagined how Susan and the children would greet him. But he never imagined what was about to happen.

"Simon, you stay right there! You are not coming into this house with those army clothes on," Susan ordered.

The World War might have been over, but Simon had left one battle only to step foot onto another battlefield: his home. Simon served only one year in the army, but this battle had just begun. It would be a long, hard fight, a struggle for survival lasting for seven long years.

There was a big argument on the front porch on homecoming day. Simon did talk some sense into Susan. What was he to do, strip down right there on that front porch? To Simon's surprise, Susan had not changed, and he was very discouraged. His homecoming was not what he had hoped.

The bishops and Susan's family were pressuring her to leave Simon. She told them, "I'm married to Simon. I love him. He's my husband, and I'm going to stay with him." She did listen to their demands and took all of Simon's army clothes, boots, undergarments, and anything to do with the military and burned them. (Simon thought she would destroy his discharge papers and pictures, so he hid them, but he never thought she would go as far as to burn all his clothes.) Now he was forced to wear Amish homemade clothes. Needless to say he was not happy.

With all the friction with the strict Old Order Amish, Simon's father asked him to move back on the farm. They fixed up the old washhouse, and Simon, Susan, and the four children moved in.

While they lived there, Simon helped his father and brothers with the work on the farm. One of the tasks was to build a roof on a silo. They had finished putting on the shingles and were cleaning up when Simon got a bright idea. Just out of the service, he was in good physical condition, so he climbed to the top of the fifty-foot silo and performed a perfect handstand while all watched in amazement. Simon's childhood happiness came back as he lived on his father's farm.

One day when Simon was in town, he bought a 1931 Chevy for seventy-five dollars. He drove it home. His father said, "What do you know, Simon finally got himself an automobile."

Susan couldn't believe he would do such a dreadful thing.

"Simon, I'll never ride in that car with you!" Susan said, hoping he had changed and would listen to her this time.

"Well, you don't have to!" Simon replied.

In her attempt to persuade him, she gave in. She found herself confused and with questions.

Simon's brother Joe, a conscientious objector, was in an alternative service, Civilian Public Service Camp under the administration of the Mennonite Central Committee in South Dakota. He needed a ride back home, so Simon, Susan, Cousin John, and Aunt Melinda took a trip to pick him up. Simon and Susan left the children with family. Four days into the two-week-long trip, Susan was crying because she was homesick for her children.

Somehow underneath all their turmoil, something pulled them together. For in that moment, they shut out the struggle between each other, shut out the bishop's demands, and discovered that they still loved each other. Ten months after Simon returned from the army, their fifth child was born, a baby boy they named Fred.

With determined perseverance, Susan stayed true to her promise to the Ordnung, even with her questions, and she tried to persuade Simon to do the same, but it was useless. He had his mind set. Things didn't get better but only worse when bishops found out about the car trip out west and the baby.

Those were difficult years for them. Susan wanted to obey the rules. Simon wanted nothing to do with the Amish ways and being bound to their rules and traditions. There was a big strain on their marriage, and things weren't good. Simon got depressed and drank more and more. The bishops and Amish family and friends invoked the shunning (meidung) against him. Now Susan was also supposed to shun her husband. They pressured her to leave him, not divorce, but just leave Simon—the man she had promised before God and the church never to leave. The Amish bishops wanted her to break her wedding vows, which would leave her a single mother and poor the rest of her life.

The Amish bishops forbade her to break a man-made rule in the Amish Ordnung, but they would rather have her break the vow that God ordained for marriages. Something just didn't seem right. How could she keep both promises?

Simon and Susan moved a lot, mostly because Simon wanted to get away from the Amish community so the bishops would leave Susan and him alone. Somehow the bishops always found him, trying to persuade him to turn from his evil ways. There was constantly a struggle in their life. It became their way of existence for six long years.

Susan hadn't been pregnant for five years, and one would wonder if the bishops pressured Susan not to have marital relations, because bishops sometimes pressure wives who are to shun their rebellious husband to restrain from such relations.

On one of their many moves they rented a basement. It was designed as a basement house. Nothing was built on top. The bishops found out they moved and visited them. It was soon after Christmas, and Simon had given his three girls each a doll. The girls were playing with the dolls when the bishops came to visit. They told Simon and Susan that the girls could not have those worldly dolls and that they had to burn them. They made the girls throw the dolls into the potbelly stove.

The bishops left feeling like they had won the victory. That demonstration proved to Simon that the Amish religion was something he wanted nothing to do with. Simon felt miserable. He loved his little girls and the dolls he gave out of love burned up in smoke. He hated the whole situation and wanted out. He would take a gun, put it to his head, and contemplate ending this whole miserable situation.

Susan became best friends with Mary, her neighbor from across the street. Mary was also Amish, married, and had a large family. They spent lots of time together talking as their children played, as they went places, and as they worked. Susan confided in her about Simon.

Mary started going to some revival meetings that were being held at a nearby Mennonite church. (It was customary for revival meetings to be held every night for up to two or three weeks a year.) She came back telling Susan all about the wonderful messages she had heard and talked about a change in her life. She tried to convince Susan to go to the revival meetings with her. Susan could see a change in Mary and was curious about hearing the messages that Mary talked about so strongly. Mary pleaded earnestly, and Susan decided she would go because she had many questions about the Amish.

Some things just didn't make sense to her either, and she hated to see her little family so divided against the Amish. She had hated to burn those dolls and shun her husband, but if she didn't, she'd be shunned also. All she wanted was to do what was right. She wanted to be right with God, Whom she loved and wanted to obey. She was only taught the Amish rules. Were they right? She came to understand the Amish religion wasn't right for her husband because she saw Simon many nights take his gun and hold it to his head. She would plead with him to put it away. She knew she might lose Simon by suicide. How horrible would that be?

She knew it wouldn't be hard to get Simon to go to the meeting because on Sunday mornings he would take Atlee, the oldest of the children, and go to different churches in the area. He was searching, trying to find answers. Susan never would go with him because she was obedient to the Ordnung. Susan often pleaded with Simon to go to the Amish church with her. Simon, in his ornery mood, would say, "Sure, I'll go with you, if I can drive my car." They would fight and then come up with a compromise. He would park the car down the road, far enough so no one could see them, and then they would walk to the Amish church.

"Simon, you get ready," Susan instructed at the dinner table. "Tonight we're going to a revival meeting with Neil and Mary."

Simon and Susan went that night to a gospel hymn singing and then they heard the old-time gospel message that Jesus saves sinners.

Susan's life changed that evening when they walked up to the altar together. But Simon, in his rebellious ways, still didn't understand all the religious stuff and was still confused, even thought he tried. He went on living his old ways, making their life a continuing struggle.

Susan came to realize that working at keeping all of the Amish-made rules would not save her. The Bible says, "For it is by grace you have been saved, through faith—and this is not from yourselves, it is the gift of God—not by works, so that no one can boast" (Ephesians 2:8–9).

She accepted that free gift, and a miraculous change came over Susan. Joy and peace entered her being, and she couldn't believe how things finally made sense to her. It was all right to have the modern-day conveniences: a car, a radio, and store-bought clothes. What really mattered was the condition of the heart, a personal love relationship with Jesus. She knew she must obey God rather then those Amish man-made rules. She was so glad she had stayed with Simon, even with the struggles.

She wanted Simon to have the same joy and peace she had, but he was still so miserable. He wouldn't give up his drinking and smoking. He remained rebellious and became depressed. After reading the Bible and hearing the messages at the revival meetings, Susan decided to fast and pray for Simon. For two whole weeks she fasted and prayed for her dear husband, praying that he would come to know Jesus and find peace like she had.

To Simon, life wasn't even worth living. He became dependent on alcohol to escape his despair, but drinking didn't help anymore. It only made things worse. He felt trapped, miserable, and hopeless. He had had enough of the battle. He wanted it all to end. Many times he held a gun to his head, threatening to take his life. Susan would plead with him to put it away. But this time he had reached the end. He was determined to pull the trigger. This time he was alone. Susan was not there to talk him out of it. But something happened inside, inside his heart. He felt peace slowly replacing the battle that was in his heart.

Instead of ending his life with a gunshot, Simon gave up. He just put his gun down and simply said, "I surrender!" He broke down and cried. He cried out to God. It felt like someone had released him from bondage!

Peace took over his miserable life. A miraculous change came over him. His despairing life started to look hopeful. His rebellious spirit was replaced with the Holy Spirit, Who filled that emptiness he had known all his life. He started to understand answers to his once-unanswerable questions. He was able to discern the difference between religion and knowing Jesus. Drinking and smoking soon became a part of the past. Simon and Susan's love was renewed, and their broken marriage was restored. They had been rescued and set free.

CHAPTER 7

Broken Vow

"Anyone who loves their father or mother more than me
is not worthy of me."

MATTHEW 10:37A

"SIMON, I WANT TO LEARN how to drive your car!" Susan said with a cheerful voice.

"I don't know how you're going to learn. I don't have time to teach you right now because of all the overtime I have to put in at work," Simon said, disappointed. He would have loved to teach her how to drive. He loved Susan, with her new spunky, fun-loving spirit; it was wonderful.

Simon's refusal to teach Susan didn't disappoint her at all. She thought of a way to learn. "Hey, the car will be here tomorrow because you're going to work with Neil. So I can learn by myself tomorrow." Susan couldn't take the car on the road by herself because she didn't have a learner's permit, so she took the car out into the cornfields and learned how to drive that Chevy with a stick shift all by herself.

Susan couldn't believe the new love she had for her husband. Their marriage was new. She was like a new bride wanting to please her new husband. Her future had hope and she was excited about this new life. She was not only excited about her new life, but she was also excited about the new life that was growing inside her. God had blessed them with another baby. She wanted so much for a boy, a boy that would grow up to be a preacher. A preacher, like at the revival meetings.

Susan wanted to share all her excitement and new zest for life with her family, so she went home to tell her father, mother, brothers, and sisters all about the good news. She told them how Simon had changed, about how much they loved each other, and how happy they now were. She wanted to tell them about Jesus so they could also have this same freedom and peace. She wanted to tell them about the new baby that God was blessing them with!

She went to visit her family that day with confidence and an overwhelming flood of joy. Why shouldn't she? Look at her life now. Look at what it was like before. Anyone could see how happy they now were. *How could anyone turn away this good news?* How could they, after seeing all she had been through with Simon? *How could they? Why would they? They wouldn't? Would they?*

The more she talked, the more they rejected her. The more they rejected her, the more she stood her ground. She wanted them—so much—to understand her so they could have this new freedom also! But it was no use. She was forbidden to ever come home again until she repented of her evil ways.

Susan lost her family that day: her father and mother, three brothers, and eleven sisters. Her family, whom she had grown up with, lived with, worked with, and loved; now they rose up against her. She was never again invited to her brothers' and sisters' weddings, family celebrations, or any family holiday gatherings.

The bishops came to visit again, but this time it was Susan they wanted to see. Susan tried to explain how different things were now, how Simon had changed, and about the wonderful peace they had. "It doesn't come from obeying religious laws, the Ordnung. It comes from a relationship with Jesus! It's what's in your heart," she pleaded. But once again she was rejected. The more she talked, the more they rejected her. The more they rejected her, the more she stood her ground. She wanted them—so much—to understand her so they could have this new freedom also! Why couldn't they understand her?

The bishops had asked her to shun her husband, and she had obeyed. Most likely she had abstained from marital relations with her husband for six years. Why else didn't she have a child those years, and why was Simon so miserable for six years that he even wanted to take his life? Susan probably never told Simon that the bishops made her abstain. She knew he hated the hold the bishops had on her, and that would have made him hate the bishops even more. Susan should have obeyed Simon, not the bishops. It says in the Bible that you should not deprive each other except by mutual consent (1 Corinthians 7:5a). After finding out what she had done to make his life miserable, she must have felt terrible. Carrying his baby was proof enough that she had put an end to the shunning. She had had enough of the bishops' demands.

This time Susan was preaching. She was venting what had been stored up for all these years. She didn't take seriously what the bishops had to say, and she lectured right back. In her frustration she blurted out, "You come here to tell me how wrong I am, but you don't see how wrong you are. You are alcoholics, and you love to drink. In fact, weren't you the one that was found sleeping in a ditch, drunk, lying in your own vomit?" She pointed to the bishop in question.

It was no use. To them it didn't matter what condition your heart was in or how you lived your life, as long as you were Amish and obeyed the Ordnung. As far as they were concerned, the verdict was in. Susan and Simon had broken the promise, the vow.

They were excommunicated (under the Bann) from the Amish church and shunned. Shunned until they returned to the Amish religion.

CHAPTER 8

Father's Requests

". . . Let your light shine before others, that they may
see your good deeds and glorify your Father in heaven."
MATTHEW 5:16

SIMON HAD DRIVEN DOWN THE lane at the home place in
a horse and buggy many times, but this time he was driving down
that long lane in a car. Inside that car were his wife and their five
children. He was going to tell his parents all about the change in
his life. Surely they would not respond the same way Susan's parents
had. Plus his family was not from the strict Old Order Amish sect
like Susan's family was.

The home place, the Mullet farm, held many good memories for Simon. The long lane led back to the homestead off a dirt
road, away from civilization. The first building they came to as
they entered the farm was the big red barn where they milked
all the cows. Other smaller buildings housing farm animals,
equipment, and feed were around the back of the barn. Fields
surrounded the homestead, with fences corralling the grazing
cows and horses.

The main house was a stone house built in the middle of the 1800s. It was sturdy and built with character. It had sixteen-inch solid sandstone walls with a two-story sun porch. Back of the house was the old washhouse.

Dat and his brothers had built that big red barn. They lived in Plain City and built barns all over the United States. Dat had met Katie Yoder while they were in Geauga County building that barn. They were married in a double wedding on January 9, 1913. The two misses were sisters, and the two men were first cousins.

John J. Mullet and Katie lived in Plain City, Ohio, after they got married. Seeing how John didn't really take to the Amish ways as they did back home, Katie said, "We better move to Geauga, or we're going to be hough" (*hough* meaning "high"— people who are not Amish). In February 1920, they loaded up his car and moved to the same farm where he built the big red barn. He bought the farm for sixteen thousand dollars, a lot for a farm at that time, but because there was a large grove of sugar maple trees the land was more valuable.

Dat's family was a lot different. Not as strict. Dat had two brothers and a sister that were not Amish. So, Simon thought maybe his family would understand.

Simon, Susan, and the children got out of the car and walked up to the stone house. They were greeted at the door and allowed in, but his parents did not help the children take off their coats or hang them up. They were not invited to come into the living room or to sit down. That didn't bother Simon; he just went and sat down anyway and made himself at home.

Talking to his parents was hard, but it was not a confrontation like the one Susan had to go through with her family. Simon said he had changed, that he was a new man.

It is hard for people to believe such a statement after you are labeled a rebel that people gossiped about for leaving your family. That act of neglect was bad enough, but enlisting in the army, not to mention all the other rules he broke, was just too much. But now he was indeed a changed man, a fact he knew only time would prove to his family.

They visited his parents almost every week, despite the shunning, and every week they received the same treatment from his parents. They were never offered any refreshments, nor were they ever invited to share a meal. That blessing was taken away. Oh, how Simon loved his mother's cooking. In spite of it all, he was thankful that they were allowed to visit and talk with them. He knew his parents had to shun them even if they didn't want to. It was those Amish rules the bishops so strongly invoke.

Simon had changed in many ways inside and out, and people could see it. One time when he drove down to Mespo to see his parents, Simon first went over to the country store where he had stolen things. He talked to the owner and told him about the things he had stolen from his store. The owner said, "I knew it was you."

Simon said, "I've changed, and I came to make things right with you." Simon felt much better that day.

One spring morning Simon got an unusual telephone call. (Amish are not allowed to have telephones in their homes. So if they wanted to make a phone call they had to go to a neighbor who had one or drive into town. Now, some Amish are permitted to have phones. They build a little shack that looks like an enclosed bus stop or a telephone booth. It has to be inconvenient at the end of their driveway.) His brother said, "Can you come down today and help Dat put the cement floor in the shop that he's building? None of us can help him because we're planting today. You know all about farming. When the fields are ready for planting, you need to plant that day. The cement truck is coming today and there still need to be some things done before we can pour the cement."

Surprised, Simon said, "Of course I'll help, but I'm sure you haven't forgotten the shunning. Dat can't accept help from me."

Simon's brother said, "I know Dat will let you help because he's the one who asked me to call you."

Simon felt that this was an opportunity he couldn't pass up. He loved his family and would be there for them when they needed him. This was a way to let his family know he didn't care about the shunning either, but he didn't want his father to get in trouble with the bishops.

Simon had a regular job at the rubber factory and was expected to be at work that day, but taking this day off was something he knew he had to do. So he told Susan to call the factory and tell them that he couldn't make it in to work.

Simon helped his father all day. He worked hard, and they got the job done, only the two of them, side by side.

Everything was cleaned up and the tools were put away as they stood and admired their work. Simon was getting ready to leave when his father said, "Simon, I want you to stay and eat with us. Will you stay?"

Something more happened that day than just a father and son getting a cement job done. They worked side by side restoring lives and building a relationship that would last forever.

Simon walked into his mother's kitchen where the meal was spread out on the table.

"Simon, you sit right here," his father said and announced to the family, "Tonight there will be no more shunning. We're going to eat together like we always did."

Delightful aromas filled that country kitchen that day, and Mother's Amish home-cooked meal had never smelled or tasted so good.

CHAPTER 9

A New Generation

Even when I am old and gray,
do not forsake me, my God,
till I declare your power to the next generation,
your mighty acts to all who are to come.

PSALM 71:18

SIMON AND SUSAN WERE EXCITED about their new life and their new freedom. They were established in a new church and started to make lots of new friends.

Simon was able to save up enough money and finally buy their first home. Their five children were no longer small, the youngest already being six when Susan was expecting their sixth child. They were so thankful for what God had done for them and for their new beginning for their little family.

Simon and his family kept their weekly visits to his parents as best they could. Simon hugged his mother and father when he saw them, which was not a normal thing among the Amish. He didn't care; love goes beyond the shunning, and forgiveness heals many wounds. They knew something was different with

Simon—very different. Was it the clothes he was wearing or the car he was driving? No. It was something deep inside him that made him different.

When he would visit, they would recall old times and tell stories of the past. They would repeat the stories Uncle Will would tell when he visited them. He had these wonderful, exciting stories from the past. The children would sit by and listen with anticipation, eyes wide open with astonishment.

One story Simon and Dat would recount was of Simon's great-great-grandfather Benjamin, who died at the age of forty-six, eleven years after their arrival in this country from Switzerland. Simon's great-great-grandmother, Barbara, had eleven children who all lived at home at the time of his death. She placed two of the oldest children, Benedict and Jacob, with an Amish family, and they were influenced to follow the Amish faith and customs.

Benedict was Simon's great-grandfather, who died on January 31, 1876, when he was only fifty-four years old. Two of his sons were working out West building barns, and when they heard their father had died, they took a train to Ohio for the funeral. They arrived late, after he was buried. Disappointed about not being able to see their deceased father, the boys decided that they came this far, so they would see their father! The next day they went to the grave and dug him back up. When they uncovered the casket, they had a shocking surprise. The body was gone. Yes, gone. Grave robbers had come, broken open only the top half of the lid, put a big hook under his chin, and hoisted him right out of his casket!

Dat had a brother six years younger named Ezra. He was in a tragic accident when he was twenty-six years old. Rumor has it that Ezra and a friend were in a dispute over a girl. Somehow they were in a car on a railroad track and a train came and killed both of the boys.

Troyer was Dat's best friend in his young adult years. They did lots of things together; they worked, traveled, and even took pictures together. On one of their many adventures out West, they ended up in Oregon. Somewhere in Oregon they went swimming. Troyer drowned and his body was never found.

They would also talk about the fun times and laugh about the happy times they had on that farm. They didn't have radio or television to entertain them, so they would reminisce a lot.

The family would get together and trap-shoot with clay pigeons. It was said that Dat was a crack shot. He would shoot from the hip and wouldn't even aim the gun. He would put his eye on the target and his hand would automatically point the barrel where it was suppose to be. Dat was good. He out-shot everybody.

They had cherry trees on the farm, and Dat saw a redheaded woodpecker take a cherry and fly off. Dat took a .22 and shot him right out of the air. The woodpecker still had the cherry in his mouth when he landed on the ground.

Dat once borrowed money from a landowner on land contract, a mortgage paid once a year for the farm. Years later during the Depression, Dat was late on his payment. The landowner thought he could get the farm back and came to the farm with papers for Dat to sign. Dat was working out in the field, and the landowner walked out to him. He asked for Dat to sign the papers. To his surprise Dat pulled out a roll of money from his pocket and paid the landowner that year's payment. The landowner went away very mad. Dat knew the landowner would show up someday, so he worked hard on a plan making sure he would not lose his farm.

Yes, it was good to take the time to quietly sit by a father and listen to his stories of the past. Soon these great accounts would have been forgotten if they had not been told to the next generation.

When Dat became ill and was dying, Simon took his turns to stay by his father's side during the night.

His mother said, "Simon, I guess I'll go to bed. You'll be with Dat all night. Won't ya?"

Simon said, "Yes, I'll be here. I got a Bible, and I'm gonna read to him, and I got a hymn book, and I'm gonna sing to him."

Simon read different verses from the Bible: "Come all ye that are heavy laden, and I will give you rest. . . . In my Father's house are many mansions. . . . I'm going to prepare a place for you. . . . Christ died for our sins according to the Scriptures, and he was buried, he was raised on the third day. . . . God so loved the world that he gave his only Son Jesus, that whoever believes in him will not perish but have everlasting life."

Dat said, "Simon, I was living in sin."

Simon said, "So was I. That's why Jesus came, to take away our sin." They prayed.

Simon sang some of Dat's favorites: "God Be with You Till We Meet Again" and "What a Friend We Have in Jesus." He sang some more of those old faithful hymns with his father that night.

The next morning Simon said to his mother, "I'm not a good singer, but I sang to Dat, and sometimes he sang along with me."

She said, "Well, the Lord doesn't care what you sound like."

His father died December 7, 1960. Simon and Susan went to the funeral. During the big meal afterward they sat with his brothers and sisters at the same table. The Amish bishops went to Simon and Susan and told them to get up from the family table and sit with the little children in the back room. They were not allowed to sit or eat with their family. How embarrassing that must have been, but they took their places with the little children and caused no dissension. They thanked God for their food and enjoyed their meal, visiting with the little children.

On one of his visits to see his mother after the funeral, she said to him, "Simon, you know I didn't want that to happen. I wanted you to be included with the family, but I couldn't do anything about that. You know about the bishops' demands. I have to listen to them."

Simon knew how his mother felt about him, and that was all that mattered. He realized the control the Amish bishops had and knew there was nothing she could do. He knew he had peace with his parents, and that was the important thing, even if they had to obey the rules and shun him.

After his father's death, his mother was going through some of her things and giving them to her children because she was moving to one of her daughter's homes. She didn't need them anymore. So she asked Simon if there was anything he wanted from his father's belongings. Simon was surprised at the question because he was not expecting anything. When you are shunned, you do not get any inheritance from the family.

Simon said, "If no one wants the big regulator clock, I would like to have it."

The next time he went to see his mother, she had a few treasures for him. One was his father's oak kitchen captain chair. It was a chair from around the table where the shunning curse was lifted, where his father declared peace and blessed him. The lifted Bann may have been for only that one time, and maybe just for that one meal, but to him it was a feast that lasted forever in his heart. A meal eaten with a blessing from a father gives strength to endure a lifetime of rejection.

Also to his surprise, another treasure he received was the big regulator clock. He was delighted with the clock. To him it represented forgiveness and love that he received from his parents. Simon prayed that the clock would remain a symbol of love and forgiveness down through the ages of time, passed along to his family from generation to generation.

A new generation with a new beginning—it was time to put the past behind and look forward to a brand new future, a future with a new baby.

Being excited about the new life within her, Susan asked God to answer a specific prayer. Her request was that she would have a boy. She already had three girls and two boys. One more boy would be perfect. She also asked God to have that boy become a preacher. She wanted him to be a preacher like the ones at those revival meetings, where she had heard the truth.

On November 21, 1952, her baby was born in the bedroom of their home.

"Susan, it's not a boy. It's a girl!" the doctor informed her.

Susan replied, "Lord, make her a preacher anyway!"

Her love for the Lord made her strong. Her prayer had not been answered, but that didn't cause her to become discouraged. Instead, she prayed that her little girl, Naomi, someday would serve God.

PART II

NAOMI'S TUCKED-AWAY MEMORIES

CHAPTER 10

Daddy's Girl

But whoever lives by the truth comes into the light, so that it may be seen plainly that what they have done has been done in the sight of God.

JOHN 3:21

I REMEMBER CRAWLING UNDER THE newspaper and onto his lap as my daddy was reading. He chuckled as I snuggled in his arms. He would give me a gentle hug as he positioned me in a comfortable spot. He straightened the bent newspaper and continued to read. Cozy, I would pop my thumb in my mouth, grasping my old favorite blanket with my other hand and quietly facing the newspaper as Daddy read. Content and snug, I sat there until he was done. As soon as he put the paper down, I anxiously asked, "Daddy, could you now read me a story?"

With a laugh he would tickle me and rub his rough beard on my cheeks. Giggling, I would plead with Daddy to stop and read me a story.

Precious memories of my childhood run through my mind, moments that are priceless. As a little girl sitting on my father's lap, I had no idea that one day he would tell me a story, his story, my parents' story.

Going to Grandpa and Grandma Mullet's was an interesting time for me. They had a big hand pump outside under a large maple tree and a small hand pump in the kitchen for water. That was very different from what we had in our home. Although, many things were different, such as conveniences in our homes, our clothes, our transportation, our languages, our beliefs, and our churches, so I guess I could say we were opposites with one common bond: blood.

I loved the big farm with all sorts of animals and being able to feed them and watch the cows get milked. I really don't remember much about Grandpa. One time stands out to me. We arrived at Grandpa and Grandma's just when they were sitting down to eat dinner, and I was allowed to eat with them, but my parents didn't. It was the only time I ever ate with my grandparents.

When Grandpa got sick, I do remember him in bed. It was a strange thing, I thought, having a bed in the living room. This was probably around the time just before he died.

One thing I really loved was in the winter when we would sit by the potbelly stove and Grandma would peel apples for me. Mom always made me eat the whole apple with the skins, but Grandma would peel the apples and core them for me.

One of my uncles lived with Grandma and ran the farm. He had children about my age, so I would play with them when we were visiting. Once we were playing with a broken swing that was on the big maple tree in front of the house. There were two ropes hanging from the tree but there was no seat. We would get a running start, grab one rope, and swing out over the hill. It was great fun until the one time I ran and grabbed both ropes at the same time. I lost my balance and fell, breaking my left arm in half. When I stood up, my arm was dangling. They say I didn't cry; I must have been in shock. One look and they knew I needed help. Grandma ran and grabbed a pillow to support my arm. Daddy drove the car up closer, and they had me lie in the back seat as we sped off to the hospital.

I don't remember much except that when I woke up in my hospital room in the middle of the night, no one was around. This huge, heavy cast was on my arm up to my armpit, and I couldn't move. I could see and hear that a man was working out in the hallway and that he looked like my daddy. He wore the same color and kind of clothes Daddy wore. I called out for him, but he wouldn't come.

Frightened because I was in a strange place with no one I knew, I began to cry. I couldn't understand why my daddy wouldn't come to me. There was an older lady in the bed next to mine, and she started to talk to and comfort me.

"That's not your daddy. That's another man who works here. He doesn't know you." She got out of her bed and crawled into bed with me. She comforted me and reassured me that my daddy would be in to see me in the morning. Calmed, I fell asleep with the lady next to me. Back then they didn't let parents spend the night in the hospital with their children. I was in the second grade, not old enough to be left alone without any warning. They had to set my arm in the middle of the night, and I was sedated, so they told my parents to leave when I got out of surgery.

Waking up with loud talk and lights being turned on, I knew something was wrong. The nurse was really upset with the old lady. She made her get out of my bed and warned her to stay in her own bed. I just couldn't understand why the nurse was so upset, because the old lady was so nice to me.

I told the nurse I really needed my daddy, and she reassured me he would be in to take me home in the morning.

Growing up, Daddy was my hero, and I loved him dearly. I loved being Daddy's little girl. He was my saint, and I respected him. I always wanted to hold his hand as we were walking or shopping. No matter how hard I tried, I could never grasp his hand. It was too big. I could only place my little hand in his and let him hold it. His hands were strong and tough from handling hot rubber in the factory where he worked.

"Nomie, come over here," called Daddy one day when we were outside. I stopped playing with my dog, Teddy, and went to see what he wanted. He was standing by his workbench in the garage.

"Daddy, what do you want?" I asked.

"Look at what I have in my hand."

I was startled. "Daddy, let the wasp go. He will sting you," I pleaded.

"No, honey, look close," he said.

Daddy was holding a wasp in between his thumb and his index finger. The wasp was definitely alive, wiggling, trying to escape. His back end was touching my daddy's thumb, desperately trying to penetrate it with his stinger. Daddy held that wasp for a while as I watched in amazement. The wasp continued, desperately trying to sting his enemy, but to no avail.

That wasp had a stinger and I knew that if it penetrated, that stinger would hurt. I didn't want any part of getting close to a wasp or a bee. But somehow Daddy was confident that he could hold that wasp or bee captive and it would never sting him. He knew the skin on his fingers was so thick and callused that the stinger would never penetrate. He had the power to squash that wasp. One squeeze and that would be the end of it. That wasp didn't have any chance of ever piercing Daddy's thumb with its stinger or of making it out of the situation alive. After I was convinced of the greatness of my daddy's hands, he squeezed his two fingers together. That was the end of the wasp.

Daddy probably never knew the impact that demonstration had on his little girl. But as an adult I know where my strong faith comes from. I have nothing to fear if I place all my cares in my Heavenly Father's hands.

There are so many good memories of my fun-loving daddy. I loved the anticipation of the surprise that he would have for me in his lunchbox every day when he came home from work. He might have a piece of gum, a cookie that he didn't eat, or a little red rubber ring that he made at the rubber shop factory. Whatever it was, I treasured it. One day he handed me his lunch box when he came home from work. I opened it, and inside was the most unusual surprise he had ever given me.

"Oh Daddy, it's beautiful. It's the biggest moth I have ever seen! How did you catch it?"

"I was eating my lunch by a window in the factory, and I saw it sitting on the ledge," he said as he tried to find Mother. I followed him around as he walked.

"Daddy, did you kill it?" I asked, carefully holding the delicate moth in my cupped hands.

"No, it was already dead. Sometimes bugs get in the open windows during the day and at night, when the windows are closed, they can't get out. Then they die." He finally found Mother and gave her a hug.

"Mommy, look what Daddy gave me! Isn't it beautiful?" I said as I tried to interrupt the embrace with all my excitement. Totally amazed with the beauty, I ran off and played with the precious gift my daddy brought home just for me.

A Dutch nickname Daddy gave me was Chumba. *Chumba* means someone who jumps all the time, or jumper. Sometimes I would be up on some furniture, perching, and waiting for my prey. Jumping into my daddy's arms was a pleasure. He would grab me, tickle me, and chase me. One time he gave me a piggyback ride; he was jumping and running as I had my arms wrapped around his neck. Losing my grip because of the jumping, I started to fall. He managed to grab my arm to keep me from falling on the floor, but the jolt and pull dislocated my wrist. I did get hurt, but he kept me from falling.

My father was always there for me when I needed him. In my dating years, if Daddy didn't like a boy, I didn't either. If he approved of him, so did I. I just wanted to obey my father.

Why wouldn't I? He always looked out for my best interest, so I always trusted him. I only knew him as a perfect daddy. So it should be. Shouldn't it?

The big shock came to me the week before my wedding. We had just finished dinner. Mom was cleaning up the kitchen. Daddy, my fiancé, and I went to sit in the living room to talk about wedding plans.

I wanted Daddy to say something more than "Her mother and I" when he gave me away at the wedding. A daddy as wonderful as mine should be honored, and I wanted everyone to know he meant more to me then just a walk down the aisle. This daddy had shown me the real meaning of life, how to love my Heavenly Father. He loved me, kept me safe in his arms, and gave me special gifts. He showed me that a sting would not hurt if you know whose hand it is in. He gave me laughter and a rosy glow, which came from him rubbing his rough beard on my cheeks. Oh, the joy of a happy childhood. I was now leaving that happy childhood for a new life. Daddy knew he was giving his little girl away and took this time to tell me a story I had never heard before. I knew nothing of his past, before I was born.

Daddy sat in his favorite rocking chair and said, "You know, your mother and I had our ups and downs over the years, but there is one thing we learned to do. Forgive each other. Yes, you have to forgive each other. That's the secret to a happy marriage. You forgive each other, not just once but always." He went on to say, "I wasn't always the father and husband I should have been."

What is he saying? I thought. As far as I could see, he was a good husband. I knew he was a great father.

I guess Daddy thought it was now important for me to know his story. Or, was he just a wise daddy taking this opportunity to get a message across to the young man who was about to take his little girl away? Whatever it was, Daddy had his reasons for telling us. I really didn't grasp the full meaning then, but now, looking back, I have learned a lot. I learned more from his story than the initial shock that my daddy wasn't always perfect.

Chapter 11

Heart's Desire

Though my father and mother forsake me,
the Lord will receive me.

PSALM 27:10

"YOUR GRANDFATHER IS NOT FEELING very well lately, so I would like to go and see him," my mother said as we were finishing up the dishes from our Thanksgiving dinner. "I was wondering if we could all go and see him today. I would like for him to see my family, his grandchildren, and great-grandchildren. Neomah, I really want us to go. He is your grandfather."

That is a Thanksgiving I will always remember like no other. It was the only time I went to my grandparents' house on Thanksgiving. Strange, isn't it? There is a Thanksgiving song about "to Grandmother's house we go." The song is familiar. The grandparents were not familiar.

Mom, Dad, my husband, Doyle, and I got our three children ready and went to see my grandfather. On the way down in the car, my mother was talking about Grandfather and commented about a Shirley Temple picture. She said, "I know I won't get anything for my inheritance, and that doesn't bother me. But if my family would let me pick one thing to have as a remembrance, I would want the picture of Shirley Temple that I remember having at home."

It was a desire of my mother's heart. A small remembrance was all she desired. She wanted only one thing, nothing more. Daddy had received some things from his parents even though he was supposed to be shunned, so maybe she would also. It was a reasonable wish, I thought.

What had brought the Shirley Temple picture to her mind? Was it a happy childhood memory? How did they get possession of it? Did she think it was valuable? Maybe it was just a symbol of hope that she held in her heart. If they gave her that family treasure, they really had loved her and accepted her after all. I knew possessions were not important to my mother, but what made the Shirley Temple picture precious to her? I wish I had asked her these questions.

Over the years my mother became very precious to me. I began to appreciate what a wonderful Mother I had. I clung to Daddy as a child. Now as a young mother I wanted to cling to my mother. I wanted to be strong like her. I saw all the wonderful acts of service she did. She went with her church to Briar Hill and held services for the nursing home. She was a member of a quilt club, and she quilted continually for the women's sewing group at church. She also helped teach quilting to 4-H girls. She took meals to the sick, volunteered for the March of Dimes, gardened, canned, and shared her produce with family and friends. She visited her sick friends, and once in a while she would even stop by to see her family. Even though her family shunned her and forbade her to ever come home again, that didn't stop her. She would make a quick stop just to say hi, to let them know she cared.

Most of all, when I needed her, she was there for me. My husband traveled a lot with his job, which left me home alone with the children, and I was burdened with the twenty-four-hour care I had to provide. I soon became lonely and tired, so I would go to my parents while he was gone. She provided me with a haven that I needed. I had grown to love her very much.

My mother seemed proud as she introduced her children and grandchildren to her father. We were grandchildren and great-grandchildren he had never seen before. I could see the respect she had by the loving way she introduced us to him. Hugging my Amish grandfather should have been my response, but a handshake was all that was permitted. We were not asked to sit down, and we didn't take our coats off, for we should not stay very long. We stood and gazed at all the things around us. Things that should have been familiar were strange. His long, white beard draped and lay on his frail, thin body. The details of his face are whitened out, for he never had a picture taken of him. I don't remember ever seeing him other than that time. I surely saw him more times because he must have been at Grandma's funeral, but sad to say, I only remember seeing him once, that Thanksgiving Day in my early twenties.

It's sad that I have no other remembrances of my grandfather. My oldest brother Atlee remembers him. It must have been when Daddy was in the army and they lived down the road with

Mom's sister. Grandfather had a peck basket, and he also gave Atlee one. Together they walked out in the woods and looked for mushrooms. When they came home they gave the mushrooms to Grandma, and she sautéed them up for dinner.

One day Grandfather was shelling corn in the granary. Atlee came in from playing out in the yard and saw Grandfather putting corn in the sheller, and he wanted to help. Atlee put the corn in as Grandfather cranked the handle. The shelled kernels dropped into a basket, and the cob was tossed aside as it was cranked through the corn sheller.

Atlee was just placing another ear of corn into the sheller when Grandfather said, "Atlee, that's enough." Atlee pulled the corn back out and the spikes sliced his index finger open. He almost lost his finger; back then they didn't go to the hospital. They took him into the house to bandage the wound and then had him lie down. He was only five years old, and I guess he threw a fit. Grandma said, "Atlee thrashed his legs around so much; he kicked the flannel off the flannel blankets." Atlee says he has a trophy from Grandfather because he has a big scar on his index finger, always reminding him of that incident.

He also remembers that Grandfather carried round, pink candies in his pocket all the time. His grandchildren would go up to him, and he would give them each a piece.

Grandfather was very hard of hearing. You would have to be real close to him and holler in his ear. He would always cup his hand around his ear to hear things.

These were the memories of our grandfather. Thanks to Atlee, we have a little view of what he was like. He must have loved children. At least I hope he did; he had a large number of them.

That day I felt sad for my mother. I could tell my mother loved her father, but there was a distance between them. There was only a strange distance of a handshake, not the closeness of a hug. Had she ever had a loving relationship with her father when she was a little girl, like I did with my daddy?

Her heritage, a religion, robbed her of a loving family relationship and deprived her of one little family treasure. How my heart ached for her. I tucked away in my memory her wish for having that picture of Shirley Temple.

Chapter 12

The Will

Now if we are children, then we are heirs—heirs of
God and co-heirs with Christ, if indeed we share in his
sufferings in order that we may also share in his glory.
ROMANS 8:17

IT WAS A DREARY JANUARY day, fog filling the fields as we drove down the dirt road to my grandfather's funeral. This was the home place where my mother grew up. When they were older, her parents had moved to the old, clay tile schoolhouse on the corner. He then had moved back in with one of his daughters when my grandmother died. It was a very large, beautiful country farm with surrounding fields. I hadn't been to this place since we visited Grandfather a few years back at Thanksgiving.

This time hundreds of horses and buggies were all lined up outside. There were hundreds of men standing outside with their big black hats. We parked our car by the side of the road. My two sisters and I made our way through the crowd of strangers—strangers that should have been our family, but they were only relatives. They were relatives that were told to shun our parents.

We sat in one of the rooms in the house. It didn't look anything like I had remembered. They had removed almost everything in the house and set up benches. We sat and listened to the Amish bishops. We couldn't see them because they were in a different room, but we could hear their Dutch voices.

We all filed through to see our grandfather. As we made our way through the house, once again I felt strange, out of place. I wondered what they thought of us. As we approached Grandfather's wooden box, I saw my nine aunts, three uncles, and my mother seated in a row. They were in order of their birth, from the oldest to youngest. The siblings were sitting in a row, and the casket was right in front of them with their spouses seated right behind them. There was my mother, and sitting right behind her was my father. They included her with the family. I was sort of surprised. I didn't think she looked much out of place, for she tried to dress as not to offend them, but she was different, much different, and everyone knew it.

I don't recall even seeing my grandfather down deep in the wooden box, but I remember the rows of uncles and aunts and my mother sitting with them. The shock of seeing my mother sitting with them reminded me of her phone call.

"Your grandfather died and I want you to come to the funeral. It's going to be a big Amish funeral, and you are allowed to go. I really want you to come," my mother had pleaded. I could tell that it was important to her for me to be there, so I decided to go. I often wondered why she wanted me to be at this

funeral. We were so out of place and looked so strangely different. I didn't want to go by myself, so I had talked my two sisters
into going with me. Needless to say, we did not want to go, but
we went for my parents.

If you're wondering why I write a lot about funerals, it's because that was the only time I really had contact with my Amish
relatives. I cannot tell you anything about an Amish wedding
because I have never been invited to any of my Amish cousins'
weddings. I don't know anything about an Amish Thanksgiving
or Christmas at Grandma's because we were not allowed to be
with our Amish families at any happy occasion.

Mother had a sister who had left her husband. Her children were grown and she had had enough of the Amish. So
she moved away and lived alone, isolating herself from family,
even my mother. She was also excommunicated and shunned.
She did not attend the funeral that day. Her husband sat in the
row without her.

My mother's family never did accept her new lifestyle. At
one of the Amish funerals my parents went to, Mom's sisters
got their nephew to talk to her. He thought he was really going
to set her straight. He told her she needed to come back and
needed to be buried Amish. To his surprise she stood up to him,
and she set him straight.

When Mother left the Amish she learned a lot about hard-
ship. Only a strong-willed person could stand up to their abuse.
She had something to stand on. She had the Lord. Over time her
family learned to tolerate her decision, knowing my mother was

never returning to the Amish ways. They became a little more kind while still holding on to the shunning.

I'll never forget all those people sitting everywhere possible, crammed in the tightest of places. When the house was full, people sat in the barn or the other small buildings on the farm, waiting for their turn to file through to give their last respects to the family. I knew all those hundreds of people were family, but I didn't know them personally.

When my grandfather Schmucker died, he was ninety years old. He had 14 living children (two had died before him), 120 grandchildren (my first cousins), 372 great-grandchildren, and 20 great-great grandchildren. There were also six or seven adopted grandchildren. They were not permitted to be considered direct descendants. My grandfather had the largest list of survivors that had ever come to the attention of one of the local funeral directors in that area.

After the funeral one of my mother's brothers gave her a copy of my grandfather's will and a one-dollar bill. In the will it stated to give his daughter Susan only one dollar. Her brother explained, "I'm giving you this now because I'm sure you don't want to be here when we read the Last Will and Testament!" She was disinherited—excluded.

CHAPTER 13

Basketful of Broken Dishes

I am forgotten as though I were dead;
I have become like broken pottery.

PSALM 31:12

MY FATHER LEFT THE RUBBER factory and was working at a supermarket in Middlefield. He would make his daily rounds, greeting everyone with a smile and a cheerful "Good morning!" Many times he would tease the ladies at the cash registers. With a little laugh, he would be on his way finding work that needed to be done. Every morning he would make his way to the donut shop, snatching a few donuts as he walked through. He visited with the bakers, complimenting them on their tasteful treats and encouraging them to continue on with their task which filled the store with a sweet aroma.

As the maintenance man, he made sure everything ran smoothly and visited with the shoppers, teasing the little children with a giggle and a pinch on the cheek. Sometimes he would cheer up a crying child who didn't get what they wanted from mommy. He would give a pat on the back with a smile to the one who was having a bad day. Many times he would see his Amish relatives and would stop from his work to chat and catch up on news.

One day after Grandfather died, one of my mother's brothers came to the store. He found my father and gave him a basketful of dishes and said, "Could you give this basket to Susan?" My father said that he would and placed the basket in his truck.

When my father went home that night, he took the basket into the house and announced his arrival, as always.

"Susie! Sim's home." Somehow, his cheerful greeting lured her to him, like the sweet aroma from the bakery at the store, and they always ended up in an embrace.

"Your brother gave this to me today at the store and asked me to give it to you." He handed Mother the basket.

She was very surprised that she would receive anything from her family. She never expected anything for her inheritance. She knew they were getting together to sort all of her parents' things, but she wasn't asked to join them. She didn't seem to mind. She was used to the shunning, or so she thought.

My mother took dishes out of the basket one by one, looking at each one carefully. With a hurt like a knife penetrating deep into her heart, she felt a stabbing pain. Once again she felt the dreadful punishment of shunning. How could they be so hurtful after all these years? Why couldn't they just forgive and forget?

A basketful of chipped, cracked, and broken dishes! It was a dagger, meant to hurt, to let her know she had made the wrong decision to leave her religion and her family.

With tears in her eyes, Mother placed those dishes in her cupboard.

One day I took my children to see my parents. It was right after she received the dishes. She told me about the basket of broken dishes and asked me if I wanted any. At first I didn't want any. "What do I want them for?" I asked.

"I don't know," she said. "I just want you to have some." There were some blue and white plates and a little bowl that matched. So I took them. At the time I wondered why I would want them, but she wanted me to have them, though why I didn't know. Now I know how valuable those broken dishes were, for inside that basket of broken dishes was hidden a treasure, unaware to the givers.

But at the time, I certainly didn't like them at all. Not only did they not look nice, but they were meant to hurt my wonderful mother. It was more than getting rid of old, discarded dishes. It represented throwing her out and wanting to forget her as though she were dead. They discarded her, and she didn't mean any more to them than old, useless, broken dishes.

The day I visited my mother and saw that basket of broken dishes made a great impact on my life. First of all, I could not believe someone could do that to my mother. It would have been better if they had given her nothing. Why did they have to do such a hurtful thing?

Second, what amazed me more than the awful thing they did to my mother was my mother's reaction. She did not throw the dishes away. She did not get angry and complain bitterly. She put them in her cupboard. Now, I am not a person who cares about possessions, but I think I would have had a little talk with my family. Or I would have decided to have nothing to do with them. Well, I don't think that even entered her mind. If it did, it was for but a fleeting moment.

Not liking the ugly dishes I had chosen, I went to the store and bought modeling paint. I painted the ugly orange chips blue. After painting the broken dishes, I couldn't even tell they were chipped. I placed them in my cupboard, not knowing that someday those broken dishes had a story to tell.

I lived away from the Amish community, and when someone found out I had an Amish background, they would say how wonderful the Amish were. Then I would tell them the story of the basketful of broken dishes. One time a friend said, "Naomi, that is a title of a book."

Laughing, I said, "I may have a story, but I don't know anything about writing a book."

CHAPTER 14

A Mother's Prayer

*Her children arise and call her blessed; her husband also,
and he praises her: "Many women do noble things, but
you surpass them all." Charm is deceptive, and beauty
is fleeting; but a woman who fears the Lord is to be
praised. Honor her for all that her hands have done,
and let her works bring her praise at the city gate.*

PROVERBS 31:28–31

AS A CHILD, I WOULD stand and pretend I was a singer in front
of a large audience and sing until my heart was content. In grade
school, when I was in the fifth grade, I had my first solo. When I
graduated from eighth grade, some of the classmates wrote a story
about what the graduating class would be when we all grew up. In
the story I was introduced and heard on the radio as a singer.

In high school, it didn't take long before I was involved in
every singing group possible. I sang solos not only in school but
also in churches in my area. I knew I wanted to be a singer, and
I knew I wanted to go to college for a music degree.

During my sophomore year in high school, my music teacher presented me with a scholarship to Kent State University for a summer program for drama and singing performance. I was thrilled; a dream was beginning to come true—what a great start. He promised me the leads in the musicals in my junior and senior years if I accepted this scholarship. I couldn't believe something this wonderful was happening to me, but to my surprise my parents weren't as thrilled with the idea as I was. You see, my parents thought it best that I not go to such a big city by myself, so far away from home. My heart sank, but I knew I must obey my parents. That was the biggest mistake of my life, and my music teacher told me so.

As I look back, this was only the beginning of many broken dreams. The dream of going to college and getting a music degree was put on hold so that I could marry the man of my dreams. But the man of my dreams turned out to be too busy with his career to fulfill my romantic dreams. The dream of having children turned out to be more than I could have ever have dreamed up. Three small children, two in diapers, and a husband who was never at home provided me with nightmares, not dreams.

We lived in a house on a dangerous corner where we received lots of knocks on our door at any time of the day. It was always accidents, they ran out of gas, or their car broke down. Whatever the reason, people would come to our house for help. Many times when I was alone at night, they would come knocking at my door, and fear would grip me. I didn't like the house we lived in, I hated the fear it produced in me, I was tired of being home alone with three small children, and I resented that my husband, Doyle, was away from me so much.

I thought maybe if I left him I would feel better. I left three times, but each time I left, I was more miserable than before. The last time I left him, my mother told me, "Neomah, marriage can be difficult at times. You cannot give up. You just have to work things out. Dad and I had hard times also, and things were not easy. Dad even wanted to take his life. I just prayed for him. Actually I fasted and prayed for him for two weeks. God answered my prayer for him."

One day while I was at my mother's, I opened the bathroom door. I saw my mother was in there on her knees praying, probably for me.

After a two-week absence on my part, Doyle called me. He wanted me to come back. I just did not want to go back, yet I felt out of place with three small children at my parents'. Mom kept encouraging me to go back home, so I went back to my husband and the house on the corner.

Doyle did realize my desire for a new house, so we planned for and built our new house. I thought, *Now I'll be happy!* Well, guess what? My husband still didn't fulfill my romantic dream, the children still demanded most of my time, the fears I had were still there, and I still blamed all my unhappiness on my husband even though I knew I loved him.

When we moved into the new neighborhood, I stopped at a garage sale that was near me. The family had just moved into the neighborhood, and the lady had the garage sale so she could meet her new neighbors. A few weeks later she asked me to go to a Bible study with her. I said, "I don't think so."

One time she walked over to my house to ask again. "Hi, I'm out walking my pet goat and just wanted to say hi. I'm going to a Bible study tomorrow and just wondered if you would want to go with me?"

"No, thank you. I don't think so. I have something planned tomorrow."

"That's all right; maybe some other time," she said.

Off she went down the road, the goat pulling her as she ran.

After she had left, I shut the door and leaned on it, thinking. Doyle was walking up the stairs, looked out the window, and saw her walking a goat. "Who was that?"

"Oh, a neighbor I met a few weeks back at a garage sale. I'm beginning to believe she doesn't think I'm a Christian. Why else would she be asking me to a Bible study all the time?" I thought, *I'm a good person. I don't think I have committed any sin. I have gone to church all my life, and I am even involved with singing in choir and solos all the time. I have done all that the church requires. Going to church is important to me and for our children. I am really puzzled.*

Yet deep inside I was unsatisfied. I was resentful toward my husband, who didn't give me all the attention I wanted. Terrible fears lurked inside me—fear of losing one of my children, fear of traveling, fear of dying—and voices of terrible thoughts. How I hated those haunting annoyances. Many nights I had to take something to help me sleep.

Knowing something was not right, I decided that if my neighbor asked me one more time, I would go to a Bible study.

She did ask, and I remember the guide saying, "Fear is darkness, and darkness is sin. Sin separates us from God."

It was then I started to think, *The sin in me is making me miserable and unsatisfied.* The following months were hard. I still could not sleep because of the haunting voices, and I continued, more than ever, to need help sleeping. Doyle realized something had to be done to save our marriage, so he arranged for us to go to a weekend marriage retreat. It was a good time away from the demands of the children and work. There we restored our love for each other. Doyle decided not to travel as much and life seemed to be better. In the midst of happy times, the haunting voices hid, only to return when I tried to relax.

I couldn't handle the voices anymore, and I shared my inmost fears with Doyle. He prayed for me. Previously I didn't want to share it with him, believing he would think I was crazy, weird, or something. His prayers for me did not help; nothing seemed to help. The voices came back.

The Saturday morning after the weekend marriage retreat, I was discouraged. While Doyle took his shower, I lay in bed rehashing all the things that had happened during the past week at our marriage retreat and what I learned at the Bible studies. *What is wrong with me?* I thought. *Will I never have victory?* Feeling hopeless, I remembered the guide at one of the Bible studies saying, "There is no fear in love. But perfect love drives out fear, because fear has to do with punishment. The one who fears is not made perfect in love" (1 John 4:18). I wanted that perfect love so it would drive away all my fears. I was afraid. I was afraid of everything. I was afraid to die! It says in the Bible that "God so loved the world that he gave his one and only Son, that whoever believes in him shall not perish but have eternal life" (John 3:16). I wanted to know for sure that I was going to have that eternal life, to live in heaven forever. Who was I to believe in? It was God's Son, Jesus, Who was born of a virgin, Who lived as a man, Who died a cruel death on a cross for me to take away my sin, and He rose from the grave on the third day!

It became obvious to me that I was not a Christian. What a big, eye-opening experience. I had thought I was for all those years. I had overwhelming fear, an unsatisfied life, and I didn't have peace about life after death. I needed to believe in Jesus Christ, Who was that perfect love, to drive away that sin in my life, and only He, God's Son, could do it! It was at that moment out of my mouth came the words, "God, damn Satan from my life!"

An overwhelming feeling engulfed me. Like the feeling I had as a child sitting in my father's lap with his arms wrapped around me. A wonder of stillness passed though my body as I felt comforted, protected, and safe. A warm, calming peace entered my soul, and fear melted away. God saved me from the bondage of fear. Thoughts of Daddy's hands came to mind, and I knew I did not need to fear the sting of death if I placed my life in my Heavenly Father's hands. I just called for Jesus Christ to save me. I asked Him to forgive me of my sin and to come into my heart.

I couldn't wait; I ran into the bathroom where Doyle was taking a shower and I stood on the stool telling him what had just happened.

I'm sure he wondered if I had gone crazy. Crazy or not, I didn't care. I knew something happened to me! The words that once pulled me down into a depression were now words of victory! I ran out and swung open the drapes. It was the most beautiful March day. Huge snowflakes floated to the ground, covering up all the dirty earth.

That afternoon I felt exhausted. It was an unusually calm feeling for me. I actually felt like I could sleep. Doyle watched the children as I rested. I slept all afternoon until seven that evening—five and a half hours! Something I had not been able to do in months.

My husband, whom I had not been satisfied with and had blamed for all my unhappiness, started to look pretty good. I started to realize it was not him who had all the problems; it was dreamy herself. My desire was new. I felt like a new bride wanting to please her new husband. I couldn't imagine living without him.

Being born into a religious family or joining a church could not save me. Being baptized or obeying man-made laws did not make me a Christian. I had done all those things and still felt unfulfilled. The only thing that saved me was having a personal relationship with Jesus Christ. God wants a broken and repentant heart. Being a Christian is not about religion; it is about a personal relationship with Jesus.

My mother had scarlet fever when she was a child, and because of it, she developed a heart murmur. She had always known she had the problem, but she had felt good all her life.

She started to develop blood clots in her legs as she became older, and it became a frequent occurrence. During one of her hospitalizations, my pastor went to visit her. As they talked she told him about my birth. The following Sunday he came and told me something I don't think I had ever heard before. If I had, I guess it didn't mean anything to me then. This time it quickened my heart. He said, "Your mom said she prayed that you would be a boy and that you would become a preacher. Well, you turned out to be a girl. She said, 'Lord, make her a preacher anyway!'"

My pastor and I had a good laugh, and it might have been at that time that I felt a calling to serve God. Maybe it was because of the new relationship I now had with Jesus. *Well, I'm not a preacher and never plan to be, but I like singing. Maybe God has called me to be a singer.*

It might have been at that moment that my eyes were also opened to see the strength my mother possessed. All that she went through with losing her family and being persecuted; still the joy radiated from her. I learned so much from her life. She was always there when I needed her—encouraging me, helping me with the children, bringing me food from her garden, making me quilts for my new home. She was very precious to me, so I wanted to do something special for her. I couldn't give her anything. She would say, "I don't need anything. I have everything I need. 'I have no greater joy than to hear that my children are walking in the truth'" (3 John 4).

Inspired, one day I wrote a song, and I asked a friend to put it to music. I made arrangements with my parents' pastor, and we went to their church on Mother's Day. Wanting to make a joyous occasion for my mother, I surprised her with a dozen pink roses and sang her this song:

"I SING TO HONOR YOU"

When I was just a baby you held me in your arms; you loved me like a special child and gave me to the Lord. As you held me close beside you, you asked the Lord to take my life so I would be a minister of God. As a child I grew and nothing more was said. I could always hear a special call inside.

I saw the love you showed for family and friends, but the one thing I remember most is the love you showed to me. The special things you did for me, the dresses you would make, the doll you mended when it broke, and the tears you'd wipe away. And as I grew up I saw that you would pray, and as the morning sun rose you'd read the Word of God.

Now that I am older, with children of my own, I pray that I'll be godly, just like you, Mom. Her children will rise and call her blessed, so on this special day I sing to honor you.

I sing to honor you, Mom!

CHAPTER 15

This Old House

*For we know that if the earthly tent we live in is
destroyed, we have a building from God, an eternal
house in heaven, not built by human hands.*

2 CORINTHIANS 5:1

"OH, HONEY, BY THE WAY, I just wanted to let you know I put
a bid on that old house down the road from us," my husband Doyle
informed me as we were on our family trip to Florida. "It's the one
on the corner. I don't think I'll get it, because I put a real low bid in.
It's a real fixer-upper, and it could make a great investment."

Our family had outgrown our dream home, so we decided
to sell. Doyle went to the real estate office to put our house up
for sale. While he was there, the real estate agent told him of
a great rental investment opportunity, which Doyle does for a
side hobby, so he put a bid on the house. He didn't bother me
with the details because he made the bid real low, thinking he
wouldn't get it. So to save the agony of explaining it all to me,
he just went ahead with the proposal. Anyway, it was just a
rental house. We would never live in it, so he thought.

Our house sold within one week, and we needed to find a house fast. Well, to our surprise we had a house. The low bid on the fixer-upper house was accepted, and we were the proud owners. Doyle called the real estate agent and said, "We may have to move into that house, so now my wife needs to see it." The agent was embarrassed; he didn't want to take me to see the house. He couldn't believe I was leaving such a beautiful home and going to such a wreck. He apologized when he met me, and I knew I was in for a rude awakening. I can't really explain how the house looked except that it was close to a chicken coop and also smelled like one. Maybe our dream house wasn't so bad after all. It was too late. We needed a house now.

We asked the buyers of our beautiful house if we could have more time. It all worked out that we could stay in our home until they sold their house. Doyle started to take the rental house apart, gutting the whole house. He put on a new roof, hauled out semi-loads of trash, and worked into the wee hours of each morning.

The only consolation for me was that this was only temporary, and as soon as this house was done, I would be out of there. We would rent it out, and we would buy our lovely new home.

I did things that I had never in my life thought I could do or would even think of doing. I will not say that this time of my life was very pleasant or that our marriage was bliss with happiness. God did keep me humble, and He taught me how to be submissive. Let me clue you in—being submissive to an engineer who can fix anything is the worst. Black is black and white is white. "Of course you can pick up that bag of cement and patch the holes in the garage wall. Just read and follow the directions."

My parents came faithfully every week and sometimes two times a week to help us with this huge project. I think my parents felt sorry for us, so they worked harder than they should have at their age. How fortunate that my father picked up that bag of cement and knew how to patch the holes in the garage wall. God always leaves a way for an escape when it's more than you can handle.

One day, Mom and I worked on a big job taking down a bedroom ceiling. Dust, dirt, and debris were falling down on us while we were pulling the plaster down. As we were cleaning up, Mom said, "What is that peculiar smell?" Then we noticed that the heat ducts were all corroded, rusty, and awful smelly. Mom concluded that the heat registers were used as a temporary upstairs bathroom.

How can a princess like me (that's what Doyle sometimes calls me) be in a situation like this? I wanted out of that house before I even moved in. I think God had me right where He wanted me. It was a good thing I didn't know that I would live in that old house for twelve years.

It was moving day, a beautiful summer day, and our house was far from done. We moved into a house with no kitchen and a bathroom with only a toilet and tub. The only rooms finished were the living room and the basement. The children set up their bedrooms in the basement with two sets of bunk beds. It was a long time before it could be finished, so we sent the children to camps, grandparents, trips to relatives, and any other event that kept them from needing to be home. That gave Doyle and me time to get things looking more like a house by the time school started in the fall.

My mother developed more blood clots in her leg, so she was hospitalized several more times that following year. Even with her illness she was still a hard worker, and she would insist on helping me whenever I needed help. She wanted to have Eric, our youngest son, stay with her while we worked on the house.

One night while Mom and Dad had Eric in their home, Dad became sick after they came back from going out to eat. Thinking Dad was having a heart attack, Mom was rushing around to help him, and with all the excitement she collapsed.

Both my parents were in the emergency room when we arrived at the hospital that night. I knew my mother was not herself, and I could tell something was drastically wrong. Daddy seemed to be all right; he had heart failure and was only hospitalized for one week. My mother had a stroke and was in the hospital and rehab for about eight weeks.

My mother still had determination and she worked hard. She was a fighter and she was going to win this battle. She did her exercises faithfully so she would be able to get around and go on with life. With rehab she was able to walk with a four-footed cane, but she still needed help with her baths and getting dressed. Her left arm didn't want to work very well and dangled by her side.

It was hard to see my mother in such a helpless condition. She was a pillar of strength. She was always there when family and friends needed her. Now, more than ever, she needed us.

CHAPTER 16

Forbidden Celebration

The Lord has done it this very day;
let us rejoice today and be glad.

PSALM 118:24

"IF YOU DON'T HAVE THE surgery, you will end up as an invalid in a nursing home," the doctor said as he was making his rounds at the hospital after Mother's stroke. My mother had another blood clot in her leg. She had had surgery and was recovering. But Mom now needed to make a decision about having heart surgery because the frequent recurrence of the blood clots made it inevitable. She knew she had the heart murmur and was always told she had to have heart surgery, but she never wanted to go through the procedures. She really never felt bad and was healthy and strong. Now it was different. She had a taste of the results: blood clots and a stroke. She didn't want to be an invalid in a nursing home, so with prayer and her children and husband by her side, she decided she would have the heart surgery.

My mother came through the heart surgery fine, but they had a hard time adjusting the consistency of her blood to the right level. She was in the hospital a week longer than most heart surgery patients, but they finally said they had the right dosage of medicine.

When we took her home, I talked to the doctor about having my parents' golden wedding anniversary party that was planned to take place in three weeks. He advised us to delay our plans. He didn't feel our mother would be strong enough by then.

After calling my brother and sisters who lived in Arizona, I found out they had already purchased their airline tickets, and they were nonrefundable. If we changed the date, the whole family would not be able to be together for the open house. We made the decision to keep the same date and prayed that Mom would be all right.

It was a cold, snowy winter day, so we bundled up Mom and ventured out. We rented the Middlefield Town Hall, hoping that our Amish relatives would come because it was close. My sister wanted it at a nicer place, but it was not close for the Amish relatives. I insisted because I just knew some of the Amish relatives would come. My sister gave in. We put an announcement in the local paper inviting all family and friends.

On the way down to the town hall, we passed the store where Daddy worked, and on the big sign by the road, they had written...

CONGRATULATIONS
SIMON AND SUE MULLET
GOLDEN WEDDING ANNIVERSARY

It was a big celebration for our family. My brother, sister-in-law, and my two sisters came in from Arizona. The immediate family who lived in the area also came. It would be a nice family reunion, with taking pictures and time to rejoice. We had lots of food, and the bakery where Daddy worked made a large wedding cake for them. The place was full of joy and laughter, and it was decorated for a wonderful celebration.

My mother sat in a comfortable chair we brought from home, and she made it through the day. She was tired, but she loved having all six of her children with her; it was a wonderful time. We had a program, I sang the two songs I wrote for my parents, and we sang Daddy's favorite song, "This is the Day." Then friends shared memories about my parents and how they influenced their lives.

Over the years, three of Daddy's brothers had left the Amish religion. One brother moved out of state, one moved out of the area in another part of the state, and one chose to remain in his hometown. The relatives who lived in the area came to the open house.

Despite the fact that our Amish relatives didn't come, many friends came, even through the blizzard. God blessed us with many good friends, many friends that once were Amish and that had also attended the same revival meetings my parents attended.

Amish bishops to this day refer back to 1950 when there was a revival movement and warn their members of that time. George and Lawrence Brunk were evangelists for the Mennonite church from Virginia. They held tent meetings in many states in the early '50s. At one meeting, they had up to seventeen thousand attend their revival meeting. More than fifteen hundred people became believers during that campaign.

Evangelist Eli Kramer came to the Amish and Mennonite communities in Geauga County, Ohio, having his revival meetings. During this time, lots of Amish attended. Many believed, left the Amish church, and joined the Mennonite churches in the area. The bishops say that was a bad time in the Amish church because they lost a lot of their members. Now, they tell their congregations not to attend any revival meetings, lest they also fall. The truth is they would rather have their children go to bars than to a revival meeting. One time some young ex-Amish went to Middlefield, witnessing to them about Jesus, and the young Amish dumped beer all over them.

Considering I have hundreds of Amish cousins and lots of Amish uncles and aunts, it was sad that only one Amish cousin came. Mom and Dad weren't surprised. They told me they wouldn't come; celebrations are forbidden. I wouldn't believe them. I was hoping that at least some of them would come. I knew the place wouldn't be big enough to hold all of them, but a few would be nice. I also thought that they might come and see my mom, since she had just had a stroke and heart surgery. I was thinking they would want to see her. They take that "shunning for life" seriously. I learned a little that day about shunning, but I had a lot more to learn.

 PART III

LESSONS LEARNED

CHAPTER 17
Detours

In their hearts humans plan their course,
but the Lord establishes their steps.

PROVERBS 16:9

THE STERILE SMELL OF DISINFECTANT and the odor of strong coffee filled the intensive care waiting room. Families were waiting to see their loved ones. I was among them and desperately hated it.

Things like this are not supposed to happen, I thought. *I was supposed to be on our family vacation in Florida, not in a hospital! The children are so disappointed.*

The disinfectant is making me sick, and I hate coffee. I wish I could have a cup of tea.

I cannot believe that just two days ago on my way home from seeing my mother, I was hit by a drunk driver that totaled my car. Oh Lord, I am thankful no one was hurt, but the stress and frustration . . .

I am tired. Really tired . . .

Is this going to be the end for Mom, or is she going to make it?

She didn't want to be taken to a hospital. She doesn't want to be kept alive. Oh, Lord, she doesn't want to be an invalid.

My mind was in a whirlwind when I was jolted back to reality with the waiting room volunteer saying, "The Mullet family may now go in."

"I don't want to go in," I said to my sister with tears in my eyes.

"You have to go in with us," my sister Betty said as she stood. "None of us will like what we see, but we have to go in."

"Well, only two can go in at one time. You or Fred go in with Daddy, and I will go in last," I pleaded.

Daddy and my brother Fred seemed to be eager for this little tiff to end, so Betty said, "Fred, go in with Dad. Naomi and I will go next."

A lady across the aisle asked my sister Betty a question. She had previously started up a conversation of why we were all in the intensive care waiting room. I didn't join in because I didn't feel like talking. All that kept ringing through my mind were the stressful events of the past week and the last words I heard my mother speak to me two days ago.

Betty gave me the elbow and started laughing. "Did you hear her? She asked if you were the youngest in the family. I asked her why she thought that you were the youngest. She said, 'The youngest always whine.'"

Betty started talking to the lady teasingly. She was telling her all about me. "Yes, she is the youngest, the baby, the spoiled one."

Spoiled one, I thought. *Who spoiled me? My brothers and sisters would say Mom and Dad did, but I know better. They all spoiled me.* Being the youngest does have its advantages, especially when we are so far apart in age. Loving them is easy because I never had conflicts with them when I was growing up. I love them all and each one holds a special place in my heart and always will.

The oldest of the family is my brother Atlee, who is thirteen years older than me. Then there were my sisters Kathyrene, Dorothy, and Betty, and next came Fred. There were six years between Fred and me. Mom did not have a need for a babysitter. My sisters would fight about who would get to hold me. I grew up knowing I was loved but also knowing we had some difficulties in our family. As a child, I didn't know exactly what those problems were, but I knew they existed.

I remember crawling up onto my mother's lap and saying, "Mommy, when I grow up, I'm not going to fight like my sisters do." She hugged me close and patted me. Without a word from her, I knew she hoped the same thing.

Little did I know then that when I got old enough to fight with someone about whose turn it was to do the dishes, there was no one to fight with except Mom. All my sisters had grown up and left home. I had to do the dishes all by myself or clean the house all by myself. Then I wished I had a sister to argue with.

By the time I remembered things about our family, most of my siblings were out of the home. I can never remember my oldest brother Atlee living at home with us. He was married at the age of eighteen, and he had a home and a little baby girl of his own. My sisters Kathyrene, Dorothy, and Betty often lived with other families, taking care of children and cleaning houses. Sometimes they came home for the weekends. If I was lucky, the job was only temporary, and they came back until another job was available. I loved it when they were home, except for the arguments. I would just step back and stay out of their way.

Like all little sisters, I always wanted to be with them. Watching them dress up for a date and seeing them fix their hair left me wishing I could look and be older like them. I always thought they were lucky to be older, to be able to date such nice boys and to marry. They didn't like me hanging around them when their boyfriends came to visit. They thought I was a pest; I thought I was just being friendly.

One particular day, something big happened. We came home from church and all upheaval broke out. All I knew was that I was to stay outside. I couldn't even go in the house and change my Sunday dress. I knew it involved my sister Dorothy, but nothing more. After that time Dorothy was never the same. She soon left home, and we didn't hear from her for years.

I knew there were secrets, but I never discovered what they were. When there were big discussions going on, I would ask what they were talking about. Mom, and sometimes even my sisters, would tell me to go back to bed or go out and play, saying that it was none of my business.

I remember getting out of my bed late one night, wanting Mom for something. She wasn't in her bed, so I went looking for her. She was hiding behind the couch in the living room, waiting for the girls to come home. She was hoping to hear their conversation when they came in, finding out where they had been. The girls were not allowed to go to places like roller-skating rinks, movies, taverns, dancing, or staying out late with boys.

There was also conflict with Mom and my sisters, especially when it came to cutting their hair, hairstyles, curlers, makeup, fingernail polish, clothes, and places they went. I always wondered why Mom thought it was so bad for the girls to curl their hair or put on makeup and stuff. I always thought the girls looked beautiful. They always had to hide their stuff or Mom would throw it away. I didn't like the arguments they had, and I would go find my daddy, crawl up on his lap, and wonder why Dad didn't say as much about that stuff as Mom did.

Now I am sure it was because of Mom's heritage; even though she left the Amish, she still carried some of the strict Mennonite traditions. She might have been afraid of what her family would say when they saw her daughters looking so worldly and going to such evil places. Mom knew the family didn't accept her, but having them gossip about how bad her daughters were was probably something she desperately wanted to avoid.

My brother Fred always lived at home with us, except for the two years he was working at a hospital as an alternative to military service. He was my buddy, and he played games with me. I loved being with him, and he was always there for me. We would bake chocolate cake together and put on thick chocolate icing. We would eat it while it was still warm with a big glass of milk. I remember that he got a spanking once. That is the only time I recall that he ever got one, but I didn't like it. I didn't like it at all. I couldn't find him after the spanking, and I searched all over for him. I finally found him in the neighbor's barn sitting in the hayloft. I just had to know if my brother was all right.

I knew there was something different about my brothers and sisters. Growing up I really didn't know why, but now I understand. My siblings were raised differently than I was. They were born into a troubled home. I was born after Daddy and Mom's life changed. They had more adjustments to make and carried painful memories from those days. At times, as I watched, I thought that it must have been difficult for them. I never had to go through the struggles that my siblings did. Maybe they did make the way a little easier for me, and for that I am grateful; but I'm not spoiled.

Whine? We won't go there. You'll see why. God had a lot to teach me, and I had to wait a long time to learn.

My son Eric was sleeping in his car seat as I was waiting for the vehicle to pass so I could turn the corner and get home. The vehicle coming did not follow the road, which was a curve right at the corner. Instead it was headed right toward me. The large green vehicle hit my car broadside and totaled it.

The first thing I heard was a shout, "Don't call the police!" as she put the car in reverse and started to back up.

I tried to crawl out the passenger's side so I could stop the lady from driving away. Before I could even open the door, three men appeared out of nowhere. One was making sure the drunken lady was not leaving, one was directing traffic, and the other was assisting Eric and me.

My house was right there on that corner, so we went in and called the police. As soon as the police arrived, the three men gave their statements and left. Thankfully, no one was injured. Shaken and confused, but not injured.

What was going on with our lives? I was on my way home from seeing my mother, and I was in distress over her condition when the accident occurred.

The pictures from my parents' fiftieth wedding anniversary party came. I wanted to show them to my mother, so I went to visit her. She looked at the pictures and thought they were nice, but her concerns were on other things. She began talking about when she wouldn't be here anymore. I was not paying much attention because I never wanted that day to come. I busied myself with chores. She proceeded to tell me that if something happened to her, she did not want to go to the hospital; she just wanted us to let her go.

Let her go? What does that mean? I thought.

She mentioned that her nose was bleeding all the time, not like a nosebleed, but just a little all the time. We thought maybe the air was too dry and needed moisture. She was going to the doctor in a few days, and she would ask him about it then. Things just didn't seem right. My heart became heavy, and I really didn't want to leave her, but I had to. I had my family to care for, and we were planning a trip. I left her with a hug and told her I would be back soon, after our family trip to Florida.

It was definitely time to take a family vacation. We had been working nonstop on renovating our house. My children were really looking forward to it, and we all needed a time of relaxation. The accident occurred on Tuesday and we were planning to leave for Florida that Thursday evening.

Thursday morning we got an urgent phone call from my brother Fred, saying that my mother was in the hospital. After being life-flighted to a hospital in Cleveland, she was unconscious and in very critical condition.

Needless to say, we canceled our trip and went to be by my mother's side.

So there we were, in the intensive care waiting room, smelling of strong disinfectant. I didn't want to go in and see my mother because she wasn't even supposed to be there.

"If something happens to me, Neomah, don't take me to the hospital. Let me go." Those were her last words and they were ringing through my mind.

My mother had died twice, but they revived her and placed her on life support. I told the doctor she didn't want to be kept alive, but they insisted that if she didn't have a living will, they must keep her alive. I felt helpless. I felt so frustrated and confused. I was telling them to "pull the plug" on someone I loved. Yet, I was trying to carry out her wishes. Mixed emotions flooded my being. Was there hope for her to make it or would she end up an invalid? Or would she die?

Oh, Lord! . . .

My week's vacation was spent at the hospital by my mother's side. We were all there. We needed each other. We needed to be strong for Daddy.

My mother had a brain hemorrhage due to the wrong dosage of blood thinner. Now the doctor insisted that my mother needed to have brain surgery or she would die. We said that she had been through enough and to please leave her alone. He made us feel like we didn't care for her, and he practically made the choice to have the brain surgery because she had no living will. We knew it was hard on Daddy, so we decided to just let the doctor do his thing and prayed that the will of God would be done in Mom's life.

When we first saw our mother after her brain surgery, we didn't recognize her. Her beautiful, long white hair was shaven. She had had an allergic reaction to penicillin and had swollen to twice her size and was covered with hives. She looked like someone had blown her up like a red balloon. She was in a coma, lying still and motionless, being kept alive with the rhythmic motion of life support.

CHAPTER 18

"I Must Tell . . ."

Taste and see that the Lord is good;
blessed is the one who takes refuge in him.

PSALM 34:8

AFTER ABOUT A WEEK, MOTHER became stable without any improvements, if that makes any sense. I couldn't believe they wanted to move her out of the hospital. She looked the same as when she came out of surgery. *There is something strange,* I thought. *They know something we don't know.* It was the sickening feeling that I dreaded. *An invalid!* Mother was moved to a skilled care facility because she was still hooked up to everything to keep her alive.

We asked if we could move her closer to home. The place they put her in was over an hour away for all of us. We knew Daddy would want to be with her every day, and that was a long way to drive, especially in the winter. They lived in the snow-belt area, where winters sometimes get rather stormy. (It's an occurrence unique to the Great Lake's states, where much more snow is dumped in the Lake Erie area than the surrounding areas.) We had no choice. That was the only place that would take someone in her condition.

Days turned into weeks. Weeks turned into months, and she still didn't show any signs of improvement. Her hives subsided, the swelling went down, her hair slowly grew back, but she had no response to us. She lay silent and motionless. The dreadful thought of *invalid* became a word no one mentioned around Mother.

During one of my many daily visits to my mother's side in the skilled care facility, I got this great idea. You know the youngest in the family can sometimes come up with some creative ideas. Mom had been in a coma for months. She could not move, but she had a little movement in her right hand. She could move her fingers. So I thought if she could move her right fingers, maybe she could communicate to us. We didn't know if her mind was all right or not. We knew nothing.

I put the pen in her hand and I held the paper on a book to control it. Then I said, "Mom, I put a pen in your hand; write what is on your mind. What do you want to tell us?"

She was trapped inside a body that no longer could reach out and hug her husband or children. She also couldn't talk because of a tracheotomy. She wrote these words, one by one as I moved the paper, ever so slowly and with great difficulty: "*God is so good*"!

How could the first words out of her be "God is so good"? We were shocked. The tears flowed as we hugged our precious mother. I could not believe her first words. Going through her illness as she was, she was still praising God. Again I saw something very special hidden inside my dear mother, and I treasured those precious moments.

Daddy was faithful to visit Mother almost every day. He didn't go in and stay just an hour or two; he would stay for six to ten hours a day. But there were times he couldn't make it. Once he had been sick and couldn't visit her for a few days, so Betty and I went to see her. We found her in a terrible condition. The nurses were busy, so I decided to take things into my own hands. Getting the plastic basin, I filled it with water, got soap and towels, and placed them on Mother's bed stand. I asked Betty to come and help me. She was reluctant, but I said, "I cannot stand having my mother smell this bad. You have to help!"

We washed Mother's face, neck, and hands, and then we got to her underarms. Lifting her arm up, we smelled an odor that was very strong and strange. Her underarm was all moist, smeary white, with raw, red skin underneath. We had not seen anything like it before. We didn't touch it because it looked painful, and we knew it needed medical attention. I was going to mention it to the nurse later.

Disgust started to well up inside me, but I had to keep going. Mother was on her back, and we wanted her on her side so we could at least clean her up a little. We knew by the odor that she needed cleaning. Betty and I pulled the pad under her and gently moved her onto her side. The pad did not come off her back, so I gently started to pull and before we could continue, Betty said, "I can't take it. I feel sick." She went and sat down.

The hurt and anger became so real I could feel it in the pit of my being. My heart raced, my neck became hot and red, but I couldn't stop. Gently I proceeded to look at the pad that was stuck like glue to my mother's back. Blood, stool, urine, and filth were what Mother was lying in. Big raw spots all over her back stopped me in my tracks. I covered my mother and went to the nurse's station.

There was a nurse at the desk, and I insisted on seeing the head nurse. She said, "She is over there by the elevator, but she is leaving for the day." I ran to the elevator and got to her just before she entered. I told her I needed to talk to her. Of course she said she was going home. I said, "No, you need to see this!"

My body was trembling, tears welled up in my eyes, and I insisted she see my mother. She said again, "No, the nurse on duty will take care of it."

"My mother is lying in filth with raw, open wounds. The stench is awful. She has bedsores. She has not been bathed in weeks. You have to look at my mother!" I announced, not caring who heard me.

Believe it or not, she said, "I just looked at your mother's records. She does not have bedsores."

"I don't care what your records say. We don't need to stand out here and argue. All I'm asking is for you to go in and look for yourself."

She went in my mother's room and looked. Immediately she changed her attitude and said, "I am so sorry. I will take care of this right away." She went to the nurse's station, put her things away, and stayed, making sure someone took care of her. The bad thing was that the damage was already done. The bedsores were deep. It was a health problem that never healed.

Betty and I trembled with disgust but tried to calm down as they cleaned up our dear mother. She had no voice to cry out for help. All she did was lay motionless and helpless as each shift passed. Sometimes the aides got too busy or they were running short of help. Of course, it would be easy to leave her until last; she made no waves. Then they would run out of time and Mother was left unattended. We knew that it was very important that we were there to speak for her, making sure they cared for her. To them, she was just another person requiring care. To us she was a precious mother.

I called Mother's insurance company and said something had to be done. They came out and investigated the case. My mother was not receiving the care she needed and had developed three large bedsores. The insurance company got her a special bed which would float her on an air bag that was filled with sand, but their hands were tied about getting her to a better skilled care facility; this was the only one in the area. We wanted Mom out of that place, but our hands were also tied. Talk about pain in the pit of your being, lasting for months. Sometimes I didn't think God cared, and I told Him so. We had no choice. We took one day at a time, and it was very difficult.

That place held such bad memories for us. The bad care was not enough; someone had to steal from us also. On Father's Day, Daddy had his car stolen from their parking lot, with his Father's

Day gift in the trunk. Once again, I didn't think God cared. *Why would God allow this? We have been through enough.* Believe me, we wanted out of there!

Even under great distress Daddy remained calm, never wanting to cause any conflict with the workers. He would always encourage the workers and thanked them when they came in and cared for her. Someone suggested we sue the nursing home and Daddy would have no part of it.

We had to keep humor in our lives to keep our sanity. One day as we were walking into the facility, we looked, and some of the letters had fallen off the sign at the entrance. It read, "NO CARE." We agreed, laughingly. It made our day, but we knew all too well that it was true and our dear mother was suffering as the result of poor care.

Mother must have been miserable at times. She had to have been, but that sweet mother didn't complain. How could she? She didn't make a sound, not even a moan or a cry. Nothing! She lay there motionless, still, quiet, connected to all sorts of modern apparatuses to keep a dying person alive.

We would bring in her grandchildren to cheer her up, but she had no response. We talked, sang, read the Bible, kept the radio on, and did everything we could to keep her stimulated. Still, she had no response.

One Sunday when all of the creativity was exhausted from each of us, I thought of trying the writing again. Everyone thought I was crazy, but what did we have to lose? *She did it once*

before, maybe she'll do it again. So once again I encouraged her to communicate to us in writing.

Oh, the looks I got when I was placing the pen in Mother's hand. I just knew Mother was in there, and I wanted to get her out. I sometimes would ask her to wiggle her toes. She moved them. I was sure of it, but according to my sister and brother, I was just seeing things. Maybe I was, but maybe Mother and I had a special thing going, and she was telling me something with her slightest moves.

Mother still didn't have much movement in her hand. She could only move her fingers in her right hand, a little. So I held the paper on a book to control it under her hand. Then I said, "Mom, I put a pen in your hand, write what is on your mind. What do you what to tell us?"

Her fingers moved. The pen made contact with the paper. Ink started to appear. The first word she wrote was *I*.

I moved the paper over a little and said, "Go on."

Her fingers moved and this time a full word: *must.*

She paused, and I said, "Mom, what must you do? Write the next word."

Her fingers started to move again. By this time Mom had everyone's undivided attention.

She wrote *tell.*

I looked at my family with amazement and said, "She wrote *tell.*"

In suspense, I continued, "Mom, what must you tell? Please write on the paper what you must tell us."

Slowly, crookedly, but recognizably she wrote *Jesus.*

Quietly I announced, "She wrote *I must tell Jesus.*"

Only silence was heard as my mind went searching, searching through files of tucked-away memories to connect with our speechless, dear mother. *What must she tell Jesus?* I thought.

A song by that title that I had heard her sing before flashed in my memory. I asked, "Mom, are you singing the song 'I Must Tell Jesus'?"

She slowly, hardly noticeably moved her head *yes*.

> *I must tell Jesus all of my trials;*
> *I cannot bear these burdens alone;*
> *In my distress He kindly will help me;*
> *He ever loves and cares for His own.*
>
> *I must tell Jesus! I must tell Jesus!*
> *I cannot bear my burdens alone;*
> *I must tell Jesus! I must tell Jesus!*
> *Jesus can help me, Jesus alone.*[1]

There was a quickening in my spirit as we sang that song to her that day. Singing that song to her was not easy. It rang out loud and clear even with our soft, shaky, tearful voices, for the words reached the depths of our hearts.

It made me take a good look at my mother's life. As a young girl, I didn't know the high price my parents had to pay for my freedom. Now, the awful condition she had to endure. Flashbacks of tucked-away memories emerged.

---

1.   Elisha A. Hoffman, "I Must Tell Jesus," http://www.hymnal.net/hymn.php/h/787 (accessed April 27, 2011).

Overwhelming feelings of hurt started to surface as I thought of the things in her life that she had to endure. Yet I was seeing a great example right in front of my eyes. She had a heart of contentment and love in the middle of hurt and turmoil. Mother was teaching me—teaching me more than I probably wanted to learn. Especially for someone who whines.

In silence, a precious mother was still teaching her daughter, teaching her in a dreaded classroom called a nursing home.

CHAPTER 19

Golden Years?

Trust in the Lord with all your heart and lean not on
your own understanding; in all your ways submit to
him, and he will make your paths straight.

PROVERBS 3:5–6

LOOKING AT MY FRAIL MOTHER humped in her wheelchair, I ached. Her head was bent low, and her short, dull hair was in need of attention. Eighteen months ago my mother was a neat, beautiful, healthy, and vibrant person. Now she looked old, really old. Next to Daddy she looked like she could be his mother. I combed her hair, propped up her leaning side to help her sit up, and tried to lift her head. She just didn't have the strength to hold it up, and her head hung, limp. I wanted to keep her in my arms, holding and comforting her, but they came to take her for therapy. She looked tired and worn out, but she had to go. She had no choice. How much could her body take?

The therapist came back within minutes and told me, "She's weak and tired; I don't think she can do this therapy. It is too much for her, and I don't think your father can take care of her at home either."

My whole being wanted to cry out, "What can I do? What should we do? Why does she have to suffer?" She was so peaceful, so calm, never complaining. I thanked the Lord for her gentle, calm spirit. I thanked the Lord we were out of that "NO CARE" so-called skilled care facility. *But what should we do?*

Mother was in a coma and in that skilled care facility for eight months. As she was starting to come out of her coma, she still could not talk because she was hooked up to a tracheotomy. She was also hooked up to oxygen, had a feeding tube in her stomach, and had a catheter. We encouraged the doctors to start pulling the tubes, but they would always say she probably wouldn't make it. We said, "We have to try something. She cannot live in this facility. We need to move her closer to home, or home, but we can't move her hooked up to tubes." So, one by one we requested that each tube be pulled. Each time they removed a tube, Mother made it through. She started to eat, she started to talk a little, and she was able to sit in a wheelchair if she was propped up.

Daddy insisted that he would take her home and that he would care for her. We knew all too well that would be too hard on him, but he insisted. My sister Betty lived an hour and a half away. I lived forty-five minutes away. We couldn't be up there all the time. My brother Fred lived with our parents, but he had a full-time job and couldn't be there all the time either. We were really concerned because Mother still needed total care. She could do nothing for herself. She couldn't even move or turn herself in bed, let alone be of some help when transferred from a wheelchair to her bed. But Daddy, with his tender heart, promised Mother he would take her home.

Mother was finally transferred to another hospital much closer to home for some rehab and training for the family, teaching us how to care for her at home. Daddy took the training and was sure he could care for his dear wife, so the day finally came that we could move Mother home. We went up to help as much as we could and arranged for a nurse to come in every day to give Mother a bath and give our father some time to run errands and get some relief.

The stress on the family was great. I had my husband and children to care for, and now my parents were in so much need of help, in more ways than one. I took over the financial part and handled all the medical bills for my parents. The amount of bills and paperwork was enormous. When I was at home, I was concerned about my parents and wanted to be with them. When I was with my parents, I felt guilty for not being home for my husband and children.

I was miserable seeing Daddy work so hard caring for Mother. He even learned how to clean and bandage the one bedsore that still had not healed. I pleaded with God to grant my mother's request of just taking her home to be with Him. *God, why are we going through this?* I would cry and plead with God. Then I would feel guilty for wanting someone I loved so much to die. My emotions were so confused.

Daddy's health was weakening, and we knew something had to be done. We were going to lose our father under the stress of caring for our mother. He never could get a full night's sleep because he would have to get up and turn her every two hours from one position to another so she wouldn't get another bedsore. What incredible inner strength my father had. I don't think I have ever seen another man like him. He stayed by his wife's side, caring for her, cooking her meals, feeding her, combing her hair, clipping her nails, hugging, and loving her. He read the Bible to her, encouraged her, sang and prayed with her. He was everything to her. Seeing my father care for my mother totally made a new impression on me about my dear father. I knew he was a great father. Now I saw him as a faithful husband who loved his wife and took his wedding vows seriously. Even in bad situations. He loved and honored her in spite of her illness. Friends and family saw the inner strength he had and were amazed. He was a man who showed endless love and commitment for his wife.

Mother got pneumonia, and the doctor said she wasn't going to make it. We waited by her bed anticipating her death when days later she improved. Our emotions were like the waves on a seashore, swishing back and forth, gradually getting rougher when a storm would rise. We didn't know if we were relieved or sad when the storm subsided. The stress on our emotions the past year had taken a toll on our family and on our dear daddy. Sometimes he would just cry. His heart was broken to see his strong wife now so weak and fragile, an invalid.

I just knew the Lord would take her home to be with Him soon. This couldn't go on. It was her wish to go home. Looking at her life, I became upset with God, maybe even angry. As a young mother, she had a rebellious husband who left her and their four small children for the army, against their Amish religion. Then when they came to know about Jesus and their life changed, her father, mother, brothers, and sisters rejected her. She had gone through enough hard times in her life. Couldn't she just go peacefully?

Daddy cared for her in their home for ten months. I couldn't understand how God could have a reason for her to be alive in such a helpless state. Now she couldn't even have an easy end to her life, but one that was long, hard, and difficult. Daddy and Mom never had the joy of celebrating retirement and doing some traveling together, as they had hoped. What does the phrase "The Golden Years" really mean?

How could God use this situation for His glory?

CHAPTER 20

Priceless Treasure

He fulfills the desires of those who fear him;
he hears their cry and saves them.

PSALM 145:19

THE AMISH ALWAYS TAKE CARE *of their own family members.*
They would never place a loved one in a nursing home. What are my
Amish relatives going to think about us if we put Mother there? They
are probably saying, "See, if you had stayed Amish, these things wouldn't
have happened."

My heart ached as I cried out my frustrations to God.

Her needs were too great, and we had to do something because
it was too hard on Daddy. I would tell Daddy, "I'll take her home
and care for her," but he wouldn't even let me think about it.

"You have a family to care for. I'll take care of my wife." That
he did. We encouraged him that it was the best thing for both
of them to place Mother in a nursing home. Yet the thought of a
nursing home made me sick to my stomach. Not knowing what
kind of care she would get was a very big concern.

Mother never wanted to be in a nursing home, but that is where she ended up. Placing her in the care of strangers brought me to tears. She was only a patient to them, one more to care for. She was precious to our family, and we wanted only the best care for our dear mother. We knew well enough what could happen to her in a nursing home.

I got on my knees and earnestly cried out to God as I had many times before. It was heartbreaking to see my mother, a total invalid, paralyzed and blind. Obviously my prayers were not being answered, so I vented all my frustrations to God. I found myself face down on the floor, resting, as I finally gave up. My surrendering prayer was, "Lord, I don't understand why You're doing this, but I trust You. If You won't take this heavy heartache and burden away, then please, just help us get through this hard time."

A few days after we placed Mother in the nursing home, I had a full day of errands I needed to get done. On my way to a store, I passed up a garage sale. I love garage sales, so I decided to go back. I wanted to take a break and see if I could find myself a treasure. I parked the car, walked up, and looked around but didn't see anything too interesting. While I was glancing over the table full of stuff, the lady who was having the garage sale came and placed something right in front of me. She said, "My mother just brought these things over and I'm just now putting them out, even though it's late in the day." The piece she placed before me caught my eye. It was a little blue pitcher and it had a white painted picture of Shirley Temple on the front. It looked old, maybe antique. I picked it up. I thought a moment.

I remembered the time my mother wanted us to go and see her father, my Amish grandfather. On the way down to my grandfather's, I remembered my mother saying the one thing she would love to have for a remembrance from her mother and father was a picture of Shirley Temple.

Could it be that this is what my mother was talking about? I kept thinking.

The Amish are not allowed to have pictures. Why would they be allowed to have a picture of Shirley Temple? But they are allowed to have a pitcher, and it could have a picture on it. Oh, could this be what Mother was talking about, and I just had a picture in mind? It had to be! Yes! It had to be this. It now makes sense.

I felt a presence like a gentle whisper. *God is giving me a blessing that was rightfully meant to be my mother's.* It was a symbol of hope that God gave to show me that He really loves my mother, and He really does care for her.

Oh Lord, You do care. You are taking care of my mother. You are in control. You still have a plan for her life, and I just received a blessing, a treasure from You!

A shocking thought went through my mind. *Why can't my mother be in a nursing home? Who do I think my mother is? Better yet, who do I think I am that God would not allow this to happen to us? There are thousands of people that God loves in nursing homes.*

As I held the blue pitcher in my hands and felt the smooth ripples of the glass, peace came over me, like calm after a raging storm. My bitterness, anger, and hurt floated away. New excitement entered my being, and I knew that my mother would be taken care of in that nursing home. With tears in my eyes and joy in my heart, I paid that dear lady her two dollars for a priceless treasure. Walking away, I knew I had encountered a moment that was planned by God and that I would no longer be the same.

CHAPTER 21

Wayward Daughter

"Can a mother forget the baby at her breast and have
no compassion on the child she has borne? Though she
may forget, I will not forget you!"

ISAIAH 49:15

ONE DAY I WENT TO see my mother in the nursing home. As I walked into her room I said, "Hi, Mom."

"I'm your mother?" Her speech was surprised and slow.

"Yes, you're my mother. I'm your youngest daughter, Neomah."

"You are? I didn't know that I had any children," she answered in a soft, broken voice.

I gave her a hug and proceeded to tell her the names of her six children. She was surprised at all the children I said she had, but to her recollection she didn't have any children.

Most of the time, Mother knew her children. Although she was blind, she could still recognize us by our voices. Mother could remember the past (most of the time) but couldn't store any new memory. The fact that her granddaughter had married was new to her every time we told her. Then, when the subject came up again, she couldn't understand why we didn't tell her before.

Excited about my special Shirley Temple blessing, I told Mom about the pitcher and asked if she remembered anything about it.

She said, "I don't remember."

I tried to refresh her memory and told her the whole story as she lay with her eyes closed.

She listened and said, "That's nice."

I knew she didn't comprehend. A little disappointed with her response, I knew the pitcher, the blessing, was really meant for me.

Each time we would visit Mother, it was a new adventure. We never really knew what to expect when we asked her questions. She was always quiet and only spoke when asked a question. She never held a conversation. Sometimes she answered as though she was normal. Other times it was so hard to hear her say things that didn't even make sense, ridiculous things. Sometimes she lived in the past and had just come in from feeding her chickens. Other times, Daddy would ask her if she wanted to say the blessing for the meal, and she would pray, thanking God for her food and for the beautiful day, and she totally made sense.

Whatever state she was in, Daddy knew how to care for her. He was by her side every day that he could be. One thing the Lord blessed Mother with in her older years was a devoted, loving husband. He was always there for her.

I felt sad to know she forgot her own children, yet I was comforted to know it was because of her injured mind, not by her own choice. Her parents, by choice, had forsaken her.

During these many years that Mom was in the nursing home, we went through her personal belongings. I found a box tucked away in my mother's dresser drawer at her home. It was a small, pretty, gift-wrapped box. Wondering what was in it, I took off the lid. Noticing that there was something written on the inside of the lid, I read these words:

> *"These were my mother's things*
> *(Grandma Maryann Schmucker).*
> *Her daughter, Susan Mullet"*

Folding back the tissue paper that protected these precious items, I noticed two hankies. Taking the hankies out, I unfolded them. One was plain white—old and worn but very neatly pressed. As I unfolded the other hankie, I saw holes, stains, and frayed edges. It had a blue border with a blue "M" embroidered on it. Also in the box was white material. Unfolding it, I realized it was an apron. It was Grandma's apron with rust stains, ink stains, holes, and places that were worn thin. On the bottom of the apron was a patch, very neatly sewn, that covered a big hole.

Why did Mother take such special care of things that most people would have thrown away? Why had she written those words on the lid? I'm sure she wanted her children to know that these were precious to her and wanted us to know whose they were, but why? Is there more behind this message than just having a remembrance of Grandma? There was a story crying out to be told. A mother was telling it to her daughter, little by little, in the silent years of her life.

Thinking back about the basket of broken dishes given to her when her father died, I started to believe that this is what she received many years earlier. Her brothers and sisters gave the shunning inheritance to her when Grandma died, when I was a little girl. They probably divided Grandma's personal possessions and gave my mother the old frayed hankies and a stained, torn apron. Was Mother saddened, brokenhearted? I believe she was. But I think she was comforted to know that apron was once wrapped around a mother who held her and loved her when she was a child. Perhaps she thought about those hankies wiping away the very tears her mother shed for her, the wayward daughter. It wasn't easy for either of them. She hung on to the only things of her mother's she had and treasured them. These things were meant for shunning, but once again inside that box was a hidden treasure, unaware to the givers. She knew she would someday receive her real inheritance, and she treasured it in her heart.

The flashback of my mother crying at her mother's casket now has a whole new meaning for me. I didn't know Grandma, but my mother knew her well. Very well! Years of memories tucked away, a part of Mother I never knew. I'm sure she must have felt the ripping sadness that she had disappointed her mother with her new lifestyle. It was a lifestyle that tore a mother and daughter apart. All the sad memories of breaking her mother's heart surfaced as she looked at her still, lifeless body.

What was going through my mother's mind that day by her mother's casket? Was it a memory of a time that they talked things through and they forgave each other and the relationship was restored? That would have been ideal, but sometimes that is not possible, not permitted. So then what do you do? Carry that burden with you to the grave? No. I believe my mother replayed that wishful scene over again in her mind as she shed those tears with restoration in her heart.

CHAPTER 22

Daddy's "Portion"

*My flesh and my heart may fail, but God is the
strength of my heart and my portion forever.*

PSALM 73:26

A YEAR AFTER WE PLACED Mother in the nursing home, I
received a call from a friend who was working that day at the nursing
home. She alerted me that Daddy had not been in to see Mom for
a few days. His normal routine was to visit her every day. They were
wondering how he was. I was concerned, so I went to see my father
that morning at his home. When I saw him, I knew something was
wrong. He was not well, but he didn't want to worry me.

"Oh, I'm all right. I just have a little chest cold. I'll get over it.
I don't want to go to any doctor. You know what they will do."

Leaving him in the living room, I entered the kitchen, praying, *Lord, what shall I do? I can't let my father die!* I found the doctor's telephone number and just decided to call and ask some
questions about his symptoms. His lips were blue. His hands
were cold. He could breathe only if he was sitting totally upright.
Sitting back or lying down, he had a gurgling sound. His lungs

were full. Of course, the doctor said he had to come in. Now, how do I convince a stubborn, dear father?

I asked Daddy if we could pray together to ask God to guide us. I finally persuaded Daddy to just let me take him to the doctor, and we would let the doctor decide what we should do. We were promptly told that I had better take him to the hospital right away if I still wanted my father to live. The doctor told him he had no choice. He was going to die, and he might have a chance if he had heart surgery. Daddy was no longer making the decisions. He was too weak.

I had a flashback of my mother going through the heart surgery and thought of what happened to her. I'm sure the same thoughts were going through Daddy's mind. The drive to the hospital took us an hour, and it was difficult because thoughts kept filling my mind.

Is this the right choice? What if Daddy ends up like Mother, an invalid? We would then be caring for two ill parents. Oh Lord, I can't just let Daddy die. I have to take him in for this surgery. Yes! I am making the right choice. Lord, if he doesn't make it, that's up to You, but at least I tried. If he ends up an invalid, well, we'll face that when we get to it. Now I am trusting in You to help us through!

Daddy was in the hospital for a week. He was too weak to go through surgery even though he needed it. They said he wouldn't survive. So they put him on medication and an IV to build his strength.

Daddy's surgery was long, hard, and difficult. As we waited in the waiting room, other doctors were coming out and talking to families. The families left to see their loved one because the surgery was over. We would ask if any news came about our father, and the reply was, "He's still in surgery."

By 7:00 p.m., almost twelve hours after he went into surgery, a nurse came and told us he was finally out of surgery. A few hours later the doctor finally came out and said, "He had a rough time, but he is alive." He told us we could not see him until morning.

Not realizing our father was in great danger, we decided to go home. It was already late, around 9:30 p.m. It had been a long day. You have to remember this family had been through a lot the past few years. I cannot begin to tell you how many times the nurses would call us and tell us Mother had turned for the worse. We would prepare ourselves and then she would improve. With crisis after crisis, I think we just became numb. I still can't believe we left Daddy, but we did.

At 5:00 a.m. the next morning, we received a call from the hospital saying they were performing emergency surgery on Daddy at that moment. We needed to get there as soon as possible. They didn't think he was going to make it. Daddy went through another long and difficult surgery. We were told that the doctor came back during the night and stayed by his side, all night long, never getting any sleep. The doctor finally decided that if he didn't have surgery again, Daddy was going to die. Going back into his weak heart was risky, but the doctor felt he was going to lose him anyway, so why not try to save him.

We called our family and friends, informing them about Daddy. The news spread, and we knew that they were praying for him. It was a critical time in his life, but we knew very well how Daddy felt, because ten years before Daddy had had the same heart surgery. This was his second one.

Ten years earlier Daddy lay on a gurney in a hospital gown with family and pastor by his side. Placing him in God's care, we all gave our love and hugs. He was prepped and ready for heart surgery. The nurses rolled him down the corridor. They were almost ready to turn the corner when my oldest brother Atlee burst out in tears. Daddy heard the despairing cry of his child. Lifting his arm reaching way up, he pointed toward heaven, giving us a reminder to trust in God. Now, Daddy was going through it again. This time he was much more critical.

He finally came out of surgery, but barely. Once again we saw a parent lying still and motionless, being kept alive with the rhythmic motion of life support. It was a long, difficult recovery. He was in intensive care for days. One day he would be doing a little better, and the next he was back on life support.

He got blood poisoning during his stay at the hospital and became very weak. I could sense that my father had given up and no longer wanted to live. A friend at my church told me that he felt my father had a cloud of depression over him, and we should pray that God would take that depression from him.

The next day when we went to see Daddy, he was not doing well. The doctor didn't think he'd make it, so they put him back on life support for the third time. We placed our hands on Daddy and prayed for the depression to be lifted and for strength to endure.

Day by day, and little by little, Daddy became stronger. He was in the hospital during the Christmas season for one whole month.

Betty and I were on our way to visit Mother in the nursing home. After that we were going to Cleveland to visit Daddy in the hospital. It really was a difficult time for all of us, seeing our beloved parents so afflicted. When Mother was ill, we didn't have to be there for her all the time because Daddy was there. Now, Daddy needed us more than ever before because Mother could not be there for him. Somehow, with God's help, we made it through that hard time.

Before going to see Mother, we stopped at a restaurant to get something to eat. Some friends of my parents saw us there and came and talked to us. They were asking how my parents were and then they asked, "How much more can you and your parents take? What if your father ends up just like your mother?"

My response was, "We'll take what the Lord gives us."

They were surprised at my response. When I had first heard that response from my brother Fred, I was surprised also, but it made me think. It is hard to accept the difficult times in our lives. We always want the good things like beauty, riches, fame, fortune, and a blissful, healthy life. We feel somehow when good things happen, we are receiving God's blessings. We don't think that the hard times can also be turned into God's blessings.

Daddy almost died on that operating table, but with God's help and the help of a skillful surgeon, he was alive. When Daddy was leaving the hospital, he left a group of people who saw a man of strength who loved God. When the doctor would visit him, he would say, "Simon, the man who came back from the dead!"

Daddy gave Jesus all the credit, and he wasn't afraid to talk to them about Him.

After leaving the hospital, Daddy went to rehab. Believe it or not, he regained his strength after two weeks in rehab and was back taking care of his dear wife at the nursing home. What a great example—a faithful man committed to keeping his vows of marriage. To love and to cherish, in sickness and health, until death do us part.

CHAPTER 23

Trust Him More?

Do everything without grumbling or arguing, so that
you may become blameless and pure, "children of God
without fault in a warped and crooked generation."
Then you will shine among them like stars in the sky.
PHILIPPIANS 2:14–15

. . . *"My grace is sufficient for you, for my power is*
made perfect in weakness."
2 CORINTHIANS 12:9A

MOTHER WAS IN HOSPITALS AND nursing homes for almost eight years. We were wondering how much longer she would linger on. *How much longer can Daddy endure this?* He was back to being himself and was visiting his family and friends, but we knew it was hard on him. Daddy would volunteer at the nursing home, bringing laughter into the quiet, lonely rooms, cheering up the old, the sick, the broken down. He ministered to the weak by encouraging them. He would sing songs with them if they liked to sing, prayed with them to give them strength, and would just be a buddy to the lonely.

The nursing home where Mom lived was wonderful. They took very good care of her. We never saw her in bad condition. She still had her bedsores, but they were under control. That nursing home became Daddy's second home.

Our friend Sharon Gingerich wrote this about my father for the *Good News* paper in Middlefield:

"Simon was Briar Hill's ministering angel. It was Simon who prayed with the residents, and cried with their family members as they faced death, illness or the complications of putting their loved ones into a nursing home. It was Simon who was family to those who had no family."

Not only did he volunteer at the nursing home, but he also found it important to visit his relatives. He let them know he cared about them even if he was going through a hard time.

The Amish have auctions on Friday nights during the summer to raise money for their schools. (The Amish schools were first started in 1950. They only go up to an eighth-grade education.) We went to a few during the summer. It was a nice time just seeing my Amish relatives, getting to know them a little, giving them hugs, and letting them know I love them and that they are important to me, even if religion separates our lives.

At one of those auctions a handsome man came up to me and said, "I hear you are Simon's daughter. Could you let him know that my dad is very sick and would really like to see him? Ask him if he would go and visit my father. You know, my father respects him more than our own Amish bishops."

My heart was touched because from that comment I came to understand that they saw something different about the way my daddy lived his life. God changed him from a rebel to a simple, content, common man. He was willing to stay in the Amish community, a town that he once fought so hard to get away from. He stayed and lived his life as a good example. He spread his love and laughter to others. God has proven that He is still at the task of changing lives.

You would think Daddy would complain about mother's condition, but he didn't. He just didn't like seeing his once-spunky wife lying so helpless day after day, year after year. That didn't stop him. He continued to be faithful to his wife, visiting her every day, seven days a week, thirteen hours a day.

Sitting by my mother's bed with my father during those many years brought us to conversation. We talked about things that never were mentioned before. Tucked-away memories began to surface and a daughter's interest was stirred. Amish relatives came to visit my mother and father; sometimes they came when I was there and I was blessed with the discussions we had. I started to see resemblances. *Wow, they really are relatives.* Slowly a love started to surface and a hard heart softened, anticipating that someday they would become family. It was in my mother's silent, dreaded nursing home room where I learned the true meaning of my life. The place I dreaded became my schoolroom. I learned things that touched my soul and things that broke my heart. Things a mother needed to teach a daughter in the silent years of her life.

Every time I asked the nurses how Mother was doing, they just shook their head and said, "I don't know how she lived this long." She became diabetic, complicating her illness, and she developed pneumonia many times during her stay. The nurses would call us and tell us they didn't think she'd make it. Each time we would prepare ourselves for her death, only to find her recovering again.

The emotional waves continued to ebb and flow. Sometimes it was calm, gradually getting rougher when a storm would rise. The arching waves would fall and smash against the rocks, causing pain, only to be sucked back out into the sea. The next round you hoped to rise above the storm, but once again you found yourself smashed against the rocks. You have no strength to get out of the situation and the storm seemed like it would never cease.

After many cases of pneumonia over five years, there was talk about stopping Mom's medication. They wanted us to decide what to do if she got pneumonia again. She was allergic to penicillin, which complicated matters even more. Daddy asked me what I thought. I ignored his questions. *How could we do that? How could they ask us to make that decision?*

One Sunday morning I stayed home from church. I was not feeling well, and once again I had a nagging nauseating pain in the pit of my stomach. Once again I was asking God to help us through this storm that was rising.

Lord, I don't know if we can take any more. We are worn out, weak. We have to make a decision about Mom's medication. It's like taking her life into our own hands. I can't take it anymore.

I was watching the television that morning, surfing the channels, when I heard a preacher say, "When you're going through hard times, and you think you can't go on any longer, you must just trust Him more!"

"Trust Him more?" I asked out loud with a desperate cry to God. "Lord, how do I do that? Right now every ounce of me is weak. I feel like I have trusted You. What's this 'more' stuff? Now we have to decide if Mother should be taken off her medication. Do you know what can happen if we take her off medication? Then we will feel guilty because she'll die. Why can't you just have her die on her own? Why do we have to make that decision and have that on our conscience? Lord, please don't make us do this. I don't like this, Lord! What do you mean, trust You more?"

As gentle as a whisper of the wind, a song came to mind. As I sang, I knew from the depth of my heart it was true. God's grace is the strength to stand when we don't understand. Oh, for grace to trust Him more.

'Tis so sweet to trust in Jesus,
Just to take Him at His word;
Just to rest upon His promise;
Just to know, Thus saith the Lord.

Jesus, Jesus, how I trust Him,
How I've proved Him o'er and o'er,
Jesus, Jesus, Precious Jesus!
O for grace to trust Him more.

I'm so glad I learned to trust Thee,
Precious Jesus, Savior, Friend;
And I know that Thou art with me,
Wilt be with me to the end.

Jesus, Jesus, how I trust Him,
How I've proved Him o'er and o'er,
Jesus, Jesus, Precious Jesus!
O for grace to trust Him more.[2]

2.   Louisa M. R. Stead, "'Tis So Sweet to Trust in Jesus," http://www.hymnal.net/hymn.php/h/568 (accessed April 27, 2011).

CHAPTER 24

Unfading Beauty

Blessed are the pure in heart, for they will see God.
Blessed are those who are persecuted because of righ-
teousness, for theirs is the kingdom of heaven.

MATTHEW 5:8, 10

THE WHOLE DAY, MOTHER WAS still and motionless. She ate a little if I coaxed her, but I couldn't get her to take more than a bite or two. She had pneumonia, and it was taking her life. A nurse came from hospice care and was asking Mom questions. She asked Mother if they could give her any medications to help her. Mother in her gentle, soft voice said, "No, I don't want you to give me any more medicine."

"You heard her say it. She is refusing to let the nurses give her any more medication," the hospice nurse announced to us.

She knew we were struggling about withholding her medicine. I felt like we were ordering her death sentence, and I didn't like it. I didn't like it at all. Palliative nursing was now being done. God answered our prayer. We didn't have to make the final decision to keep giving her medicine to prolong her life.

Medicine has become so difficult at times, and you wonder, *What is right?* Questions arise, emotions wear thin, and then guilt and pain enter one's being. Our hearts were torn seeing a loved one suffering and now dying. Oh, to avoid the pain!

Mother had taught me things all my life, how to love my husband and raise my children. Now she was teaching me in her silence about the final stages of life, the inevitable, that one is destined to die, to gracefully let go of life so you can be released into God's care.

In the restful moments of the day I would sing to her.

With her quiet, soft voice she would join in. One thing always amazed me about Mother. She sometimes would forget who her children were, she sometimes thought she was at home and Dad was in the barn feeding her chickens; she would mix up all sorts of things. But there were some things she would never forget, like the Bible verses she memorized and the hymns she learned to love. All you would have to do was ask her if she knew a verse. If she did, she would say it from memory. Then when you started to sing, she would sometimes join in. She had hidden God's Word in her heart. Down deep inside, my mother had a hidden treasure.

On the outside, my mother was old, broken down, paralyzed, and blind, but hidden on the inside was her unfading beauty, imperishable quality, and the lasting charm of a gentle and quiet spirit, which is so precious and of great worth in the sight of God (1 Peter 3:4).

Daddy stayed by Mother's side all day long, hugging her, praying with her, reassuring her of his love. Daddy would just cry and then say, "She has suffered so long. As much as I want her to be with me, I have to let her go." Daddy took care of Mother for more than four years after his heart surgery. It was a long, drawn-out period in our lives.

I really believe that Mother's long illness saved our father. If Mother had died suddenly, I truly believe he would have gone soon after because of a broken heart. Dad and Mom had a bond for fifty years. They went through a lot together, and Daddy was dependent upon her. Then seven years of caring for her during her illness gave him time to adjust and then ability to release her.

Later on that evening, I was singing to her when my brother Fred walked into the room. He interrupted me because he had something to ask me concerning letting our siblings know what was going on. We were talking, and as we were finishing, we noticed Mother was still singing the song I had sung to her, all by herself with her quiet, soft, broken voice.

"What a day that will be,
When my Jesus I shall see,
And I look upon His face,
The One who saved me by His grace;
When He takes me by the hand,
And leads me through the Promised Land,
What a day, glorious day that will be."

We stayed in Mother's room all night long. Daddy slept on a lounge chair, and I was in the bed next to Mom. My thoughts and emotions were running wild as I was lying there quietly. It was difficult to fall asleep because I would check each movement that was made. Mostly it was Daddy or the nursing home staff in the hallway. Mother was quiet all night except for her heavy breathing and the sound of the oxygen so she could breathe somewhat easier.

Early in the morning Mother responded a little, and again Daddy reassured her of his love. He said, "Susie, I have to say goodbye, but we will meet again." She nodded her head. Slowly she slipped away. Only her labored breathing let us know she was still alive. The day was long and hard. We knew that soon a loved one would be gone.

With her final breath that evening, Jesus came, took my mother by her hand, and led her to that Promised Land.

There is coming a day,
When no heart aches shall come,
No more clouds in the sky,
No more tears to dim the eye,
All is peace forever more
On that happy golden shore,
What a day, glorious day that will be.

What a day that will be,
When my Jesus I shall see,
And I look upon His face,
The One who saved me by His grace;
When He takes me by the hand,

And leads me through the Promised Land,
What a day, glorious day that will be.

There'll be no sorrow there,
No more burdens to bear,
No more sickness, no pain,
No more parting over there;
And forever I will be,
With the One who died for me,
What a day, glorious day that will be.[3]

3.   Jim Hill, "What a Day That Will Be," http://preciouslordtakemyhand.com/publish/
christianhymns/what-a-day-that-will-be/ (accessed April 27, 2011).

CHAPTER 25

Brokenness Mended

Be kind and compassionate to one another,
forgiving each other, just as in Christ God forgave you.
EPHESIANS 4:32

SIX CHILDREN AND A FATHER gathered around a casket viewing their precious mother and wife. We were holding each other in a close embrace, united in the same feeling of loss. Though our lives had taken different directions and we lived miles apart, we were drawn together as one. We felt a common bond of love and togetherness. Words were softly spoken as we remembered our dear mother's life.

Daddy in his tender spirit said, "Please forgive me for not always being the father that I should have been to you children." I thought to myself, *Where did that come from? My daddy?* He was my perfect father. I had heard that shocking phrase once before when he told me his life story right before my wedding. Oh yes, I knew he was human and he made mistakes, but to me he was my perfect daddy.

Then my oldest brother responded, "Dad, that's all right. None of us are perfect parents like we hope to be. We've all done things we're not proud of."

Flashbacks came of the story Daddy told me about his life before I was born. I only knew my *good* daddy; my brothers and sisters had known my *other* daddy—the Amish rebel. They were raised in a troubled, stressed-out home with strict rules and traditions. The wonder of it all! God takes broken lives and broken families and mends them back together with forgiveness.

As our arms released the embrace, Dorothy bent down burying her face, crying on Mom. Once again I found myself seeing a loved one crying in front of a casket, not really knowing what those tears meant.

The next morning was Mother's funeral. Our family gathered at our parents' home, where we held a private service. We were singing and sharing precious memories of Mother. I shared the story of the basket of broken dishes with the impression that my family knew the story. I thought that Mother must have told them. To my surprise, it was news to all except Dad and Fred. Some of the children had moved to Arizona when this all happened, and Mother never told them.

Kathy began to cry. "Mom's sisters really didn't do that to her, did they? How could they give Mom broken dishes for her inheritance? They were at the viewing yesterday and were all crying. If they did that, it seems like they don't even like her, so why were they crying?"

Daddy said, "Actually, they might have cried because they were sad that their sister was not Amish when she died."

I then remembered a time that Daddy told me about a visit he had from one of Mom's brothers. Mom's sister (the one who left the Amish and her family) returned to her husband when she found out she had cancer. She died and was then buried Amish.

During the time of their sister's funeral, Mom's brother, who was a bishop, visited my parents at the nursing home. He tried to convince Dad to return to the Amish so Mom could be buried Amish when the time came, just like his other sister. "You know, you can still turn back so Sue can be Amish when we bury her," he said. (They believe when you die if you are not buried Amish, you are doomed, cut off from God.)

Daddy had replied, "You don't have to be buried in Amish clothes to be sure you go to heaven. What matters is what condition your heart is in." After that visitation from her brother, Daddy had a concern that if he died first, they would want to bury her Amish when she died.

What mixed up feelings we were experiencing that morning. Kathy, still crying, said, "Mom's sisters look so much like Mom. I hugged each of them yesterday. How could they do that to our mother?" Her tears flowed, and we could tell Kathy was bitterly hurt.

We all tried to encourage her. Mother never really believed it was her sisters but her brothers who gave her the broken dishes. They were bishops in the Old Order Amish church, one of the strictest sects. They had to make sure the shunning was carried through for life. I'm sure it must have hurt Mom, but she knew what God was asking her to do: forgive them and not hold a grudge.

In Mom's Bible she wrote these words, "Forgive and you will be forgiven. Ask God to bless the person that you have something against. The blessing will fall on you." Forgiveness mended the hurt intended by the broken dishes, and Mother forgave her siblings in her heart. That's why she could place those broken dishes in her cupboard with love instead of bitterness.

Mother would always talk about her sisters in a positive way. She loved them. She would never want her children to feel bad about her family. Her sisters would sometimes come and visit her when she was in the hospital. I remember one time when most of her sisters came after she had her first stroke. I couldn't believe she had so many sisters. There were twelve girls in that family.

The funeral was over and our family and friends were filing through to show their last respects. Four of Mother's sisters came forward, and together they were viewing and crying at Mother's casket. At that moment, everyone in our immediate family thought of Kathy and her bitter feelings. As the sisters started to leave, we heard a cry. It was Kathy. She was weeping, loudly and deeply. Kathy got up, embraced each of her four aunts one at a time, telling each she loved them, and gave each a kiss. Only the family members knew what that moment really meant.

We invited all of our Amish family to stay for the meal in our church's fellowship hall, but they all left. Funny, isn't it? We can stay and eat at the Amish funerals (although we have to eat alone at separate tables), but the Amish are not allowed to stay and eat at our meals at all. They have to obey the Ordnung and shun us, even at death.

 PART IV

PURPOSES REVEALED

CHAPTER 26

Traditions

Jesus said to her, "I am the resurrection and the life.
The one who believes in me will live, even though
they die; and whoever lives by believing in me will
never die. Do you believe this?"

JOHN 11:25–26

MY FATHER'S AMISH SISTER DIED in March of 1995, two months after Mother died. Daddy wanted to go to the funeral, and he asked if I would take him to Pennsylvania. Seeing some of my Amish relatives at my mother's funeral gave me a new view of my heritage. I was interested in learning more. So I took my twelve-year-old son, Eric, out of school to go to this once-in-a-lifetime event because I thought this would be a great learning experience for him. Actually I was surprised at my reaction about wanting to go, since I never liked the experience. Knowing Daddy wanted to go and knowing he didn't want to go by himself made the trip worthwhile.

We drove the three hours to Pennsylvania. There was no snow but it was dreary and cloudy. At times a light, misty rain fell. On the way, Daddy was concerned about how to get through a certain town because our map didn't have details of the town. As we were just entering the town, Daddy said, "Look for a Bob's Big Boy restaurant. The Amish say they usually stop there to eat." When the Amish travel from one Amish community to another, they get a large group together and have a taxi drive them. That restaurant was a stopping point for that particular trip.

As we were driving past the restaurant, I saw a van full of Amish just leaving. Daddy said, "Follow them. I'm sure they are going to the funeral." We followed them for about forty-five minutes, and, yes, they were going to the same funeral. As we drove up to the farm where my aunt lived, we saw rows of buggies and across the street about twenty-five large vans were parked. We parked our car and started to walk across the street when I saw one of my uncles and his family drive up. We waited for them because we really didn't want to walk in by ourselves. They were Conservative-Mennonite, not Amish. They dressed very plain, similar to the Amish dress, but I still felt better that I knew someone there. He was my uncle who lived by my grandpa and grandma Mullet's, and we visited them when I was a child. I was thrilled when my uncle and his family drove in since I didn't know any of the other people there.

We walked together to the entrance of the house. Amish men with their wide-rimmed hats were standing in front of the buggies. The horses weren't there. I don't know where they put the horses, maybe tied up at a hitching post somewhere or in the barn. A big man came to the door and asked in Dutch, "Veah bist du [Who are you]?"

My aunt replied, "Des sind irrea breedah, und ich bin sie frau [These are brothers, and I'm his wife]."

"Komm mich noch [Follow me]," he said, leaving the rest of us waiting out on the steps. He came back and motioned for us to follow him. He didn't even ask who we were. My son Eric and my female cousins followed me. The men stayed behind.

The big man, the Amish funeral director, motioned for me to sit on a long bench against the far wall. We sat, and then I saw rows of women dressed in black dresses with white kapps, and it hit me. Eric was a boy and he should have stayed with my men cousins, but he didn't know. I never thought of sending him with them. I felt out of place in more ways than one.

It was 9:15 a.m. The rooms were filled with people, and the house was still and strange. Except for the funeral director who took care of all the funeral arrangements, no one spoke as he moved around and told people where to sit.

At 9:30 a bishop got up and spoke in German, so it was difficult for me to understand. At one point, I understood he was talking about Cain and Abel. Later on I knew he quoted, "In my Father's house are many mansions, and if I go and prepare a place for you, I will come and receive you unto myself, that where I am you may be also." I wondered if he really believed what he just quoted. I didn't know how that related to Cain and Abel, but nothing made sense to me.

He had a handkerchief cupped in his hand and would hold it to his mouth when he coughed, which was about every other minute. I thought maybe it was his personal style. Maybe it was a habit, because it didn't sound like an illness or a hoarse throat.

At one point Eric leaned over and said, "Mom, what's he doing now?" Anyone could tell it was something different. Like a sing-song chant. I guess he was quoting something from memory. I didn't know what he was saying. I leaned over to my cousin Betty Ann and asked her if she understood everything because she was raised Amish and left the Amish after she was older.

She said, "Not all."

I was relieved because I thought I was good at understanding Dutch, but that bishop was difficult to understand. He was about eight feet away from me, leaning on the side of the door at the entrance to the main room and the large kitchen where I was sitting.

I could see into the next room and had noticed the end of my aunt's pine box casket, held up by two chairs. Sitting behind the casket were her husband, children, grandchildren, then brothers and sisters. That's the room my father was in, but I couldn't see him. All the rooms were packed with rows and rows of Amish church benches. Far on the other side of the kitchen was a big porch that was full of women, and the basement was full of women, children, and older men. I don't believe they could hear the bishop if I had a difficult time understanding him under his soft rumble. They didn't even act as though they were trying to hear. They were content just being there, pretending to listen.

Chapter 27

Plain Adornment

Clearly no one who relies on the law is justified before
God, because "the righteous will live by faith."

GALATIANS 3:11

I LOOKED AT THE ROWS of women all wearing their black
funeral dresses and sitting on benches with arched backs. They were
dressed in very plain and simple clothes without any individuality,
all identical. There was a feeling of extravagant devotion. Yet I felt
a sense of self-assurance that their plain adornment was far better
than mine.

There were some women with babies, and I noticed a little
girl about five years old sitting by her mother. Not once did
I see her ask her mother a question or squirm for the whole
three hours we sat there. One time she leaned her head on her
mother's shoulder, but only for a few minutes. I wondered how
they train them.

A baby next to me with a black dress and a crocheted bib
started to cry. The young mother tried everything to quiet her,
but she didn't respond. The mother took a bottle out of her

Amish-black diaper bag. It was a little dropper bottle, like those you get babies' vitamins in. The bottle was unmarked and all the paper was taken off, but she gave the baby two droppers full of whatever it was.

My cousin Betty Ann leaned over and said, "That's a boy."

I looked at her and said, "How do you know?"

"All the Amish baby girls wear little kapps. That baby has no kapp on. Believe it or not, the Amish baby boys wear dresses."

I leaned over to tell Eric, and his eyebrows went up in surprise. The mother took the baby out. There was a door to the outside right behind her. She came back in about fifteen minutes without the baby. She must have put him down to sleep somewhere outside in one of the buildings on the farm.

After about forty-five minutes, the bishop sat down. It was very still and quiet in all the rooms. I saw another man who was a preacher or a bishop stand up very slowly with a handkerchief cupped in his hand. He cleared his throat twice with a sickening sound, like a child when he is pretending he has a cough and wants attention. He leaned against the door entrance, moving slowly back and forth like a caterpillar crawling. He started to talk with his head bent down like in prayer, but I didn't see anyone else acting like they were praying. He had his eyes shut, head bowed, and was leaning against the door entrance. The handkerchief was cupped in his hand and held in front of his mouth when he coughed. He slightly moved his hand forward when he talked. That was the position he was in the whole hour he spoke. Like the other bishop, he coughed about every minute also. I was beginning to believe that was a requirement to be an Amish leader in this area.

About 11:45 a.m., a little movement started, and I knew something different was going to happen, but I didn't understand.

My cousin, Betty Ann, said, "We have to kneel to pray."

We all knelt and the bishop prayed this sing-song prayer. I didn't know if he was reading the prayer or if it was memorized. Then we all stood. The bishop was quoting something from memory and at two certain times all the people bent their knees slightly, like a curtsy. Later I asked my cousin what that was all about. She explained that when Christ's name is spoken, they bend their knees in honor to Him.

We all sat down when the bishop was done. The funeral director got up and walked out of the room down through the porch into the basement. About five minutes later men started to come out of the basement, through the porch, and outside. They walked along the side of the house to the side door where we were seated.

The funeral director led them in right by us. We had to move our legs as far back as we could to let them through. He led them through the doorway where the preachers stood, and in front of my aunt's casket to view the body. He then led them out through the kitchen, through the porch, to the outside. Then he went and got another group.

To my surprise, people were coming from some place outside, maybe the barn or other buildings; I don't know, but there were hundreds. They walked right by me, so I looked them up and down and tried to count each one there. In wonder, I thought, *These people are relatives but strangers to me.*

The men all wore blue with wide-rimmed black hats. All their clothes were home-sewn. Many of the clothes looked tight, uncomfortable. I noticed the pants would pull at certain areas. They were tight around the hips, with lots of folds on the bottom of their seat. Being able to sew, I know how uncomfortable some homemade pants are, and I tell you, those pants looked uncomfortable. All the boys around twelve years old wore straw hats. Younger boys wore blue stocking hats. They took off their hats as they entered the house.

As the men and boys were passing by us, I noticed how dirty their clothes were. I thought that they must have been sitting in the barn, but I noticed that the dirt didn't come from just that day. It was dirt that had been there for a long time, and I was wondering when they last washed their clothes. It was a common thing. All the men's clothes looked dirty and grubby with grime, horsehair, and holes. Some of them must have left work in the barns and come straight to the funeral without changing. All the men had long beards. The hair on their head was long and matted down in a rim around their heads created from their hats. I looked at their big black-rimmed hats as they took them off because they held them right in front of my face. Many of the hats were also dirty. I tried to look and see if they marked their hats in some way so they could tell them apart, but I couldn't see any markings, except for dirt.

As the women, girls, and women with their babies walked by, they looked much cleaner, but some of their black shawl blankets looked worn. I did see that many had them marked with either their name or initials embroidered in them so they could tell them apart. All the women had on black dresses which were closed with straight pins, black stockings, black shoes, and black jackets with hooks and eyes (no buttons) worn under their blankets. The shawl blankets were folded in half, laid on their shoulders, and fastened with a regular large diaper pin to hold them on at the neck. The women and baby girls wore white kapps, and the little girls wore black kapps made the same as the white kapps. The girls wear black kapps until they become members in the Amish church, then they wear white.

Chapter 28

My Heritage

It is for freedom that Christ has set us free. Stand firm,
then, and do not let yourselves be burdened again by a
yoke of slavery.

Galatians 5:1

I WONDERED WHERE ALL THESE people came from because there were lots of men. "Do they all take a day off from work for funerals?" I asked Daddy after the funeral.

"It is an Amish pastime to go to funerals," he laughingly replied and then said respectfully, "No, they just have lots of relatives."

On my mother's side alone I have around 120 first cousins, and now I also have around 770 first cousins once removed. Obviously, my father has a big family also. On his side, I have around 76 first cousins. From both sides of the family, I had 25 uncles and aunts, not including their spouses, 11 on my father's side, and 14 on my mother's side. Maybe that's why they have such big attendance at funerals. I had counted around 500 people when it was time for us to get up and view the body. I saw the packed rooms where I couldn't count and figured there were around another 100 people in the crowded living room and bedroom that was off to the side.

As I walked past my aunt's casket, I was thinking, *Here is my aunt, and I probably have never met or seen her before.* I didn't even know her. She was a small, pretty lady who looked young. I found out she was only fifty-nine, and she died from cancer. She had on a dark-colored dress with a nice white apron and a bodice on top that was worn for special occasions. She had on a white Amish kapp with ribbon that tied around her neck in a bow.

We walked out to the back porch, and there we waited for all the others to pass by. The men stood outside in the cold, and the women stayed inside the house. After about half an hour, we heard a mumble, and it was the familiar sound in the distance of the preachers speaking, but we couldn't understand. We waited a while, and then they brought her casket out and put it in a special Amish buggy that was made longer to carry caskets.

As we were getting ready to get in our car to drive to the graveyard, a young Amish man came up to me and said, "I don't know you. Who are you?"

I said, "I am Simon Mullet's daughter."

To my surprise, he replied, "You're Neomah?"

"Yes, and who are you?" I replied.

He was my aunt's son, my first cousin. I wondered how he knew me after I said my father's name. How did he know my name?

I then remembered at my mother's funeral a woman about my age came to me and asked me if I knew her. I looked at her and saw a total stranger. I had felt I had never seen her before in my life. I said, "No. I'm sorry, I don't."

"Well, I know you," she said. "You used to ride on my bus when we were little. You would get on the bus, and I would watch you. You are my first cousin!" I gave her a big hug. "I'm now like you," she said. "I'm a Christian."

Families started getting into their buggies. Some men hitched up their horses while they were waiting. They started the funeral procession. Lots of Amish who had come by taxi also got into their vans and the driver drove them to the graveyard, which was on my aunt's property, down the road off a side street.

As we entered the graveyard, it was by an open cornfield on top of a large hill. Down the side were trees and the beginning of hills; you could see the top of the hillsides across many acres. It was a beautiful view even on that day with its cold wintry look and the foggy, misty clouds over the hillsides.

The Amish started gathering in groups in a very large circle around the casket. There was a large group of men on the west side and women on the east side. Immediate family were in one group with smaller groups of men and other groups of women scattered around the large circle.

Four pallbearers took the casket and placed it on two chairs. The funeral director opened the casket, got an umbrella and held it over the body, and motioned for a group of men to come and view the body. We all filed past the casket once again.

People went back to their groups in a large circle. Then the immediate family went up to view their loved one for the last time. All looked on from a distance as the family cried and sounds of heartache filled the hillsides.

The funeral director closed the lid to the casket, and as the family stood close and watched, he screwed the lid shut. The pallbearers picked up the casket and placed it on two boards that were over the grave. They placed two straps under the casket. As four men held the ends of the straps, two other men took away the two boards. The men holding the straps lowered the casket down into another pine box in the grave. Then they lowered the lid to the pine box vault.

The pallbearers took shovels and started covering the box with dirt as the bishops started to sing-song chant. We could barely hear them, let alone understand what they were singing. Then a group of men on the west started chanting along with the bishop. At times you would hear only the bishop's voice, and then the group of men would echo back.

When the four men were tired of shoveling, another group of four men came and took the shovels and continued filling the grave. The singing and filling of the grave went on for about half an hour until the grave was covered. The men patted the grave with the backs of their shovels, and then the bishop said something we couldn't hear. When it was all over, the bishop got out his pipe, lit it, and started smoking.

The groups of people started to talk and move, but they stayed a long while, still talking.

I looked at the whole picture, the view on the hill with groups of women with black on and men with blue color all over. It was a beautiful sight, this picture of a group of people pulled together in one accord. I wondered what they felt. Did they really want to live as they do, or did they live like that out of fear, with no hope? My heart ached as I wondered what this group of relatives, hundreds of them, thought of my father and me.

Daddy and I really stood out on that hillside dotted in black and blue. We were definitely different. Daddy had on a gray suit with a gray hat. I wore a black dress but forgot that my green coat would be standing out in splendid color on the gray winter day surrounded by all that black and dark navy blue. We looked different, but what I hoped they could see was something different inside us. I wanted to shout and tell them that we can know for sure that we are going to heaven when we die, that we don't have to hope that we are good enough. Jesus took care of that for us. My heart ached as I thought that right in front of me were my relatives and I could have been one of them, just like them, in bondage, burdened with man-made laws.

As I was leaving, a cousin came up to me and asked, "Do you remember me?"

I looked at her and said, "You look familiar. I'm sure you are my cousin, but I don't know who you are." I had figured it out. If I said someone was my first cousin, chances were I would be right.

She said, "Yes, I am your first cousin Cathy. I live at the end of the lane where Grandpa and Grandma lived. Every time you came down to see Grandpa and Grandma I would ask my mother if I could go and play with you; sometimes she would let me, and when she did, I was so glad." As we talked, others walked by nodding as if to say hi and smiled.

Another cousin approached me. She introduced herself and told me she was related to me on my mother's side and also on my father's side. When she told me her last name was the same as mine, I thought she was going to say she was also related to my husband. Not surprising to me, I suspect that she probably was.

A few more cousins came and introduced themselves to me, and then my three aunts came. I talked to them and asked if one of them was the sister my dad had picked on by messing up her kapp right after she got done making it. They all said no. Just then Daddy came around the corner, and he said it was his oldest sister.

Another cousin came up to me and introduced herself and said, "When articles and pictures of you were in the paper, I would clip them and put them in a scrap book, and I still have them."

I was amazed that someone I hardly remembered would do that. What had I done for her to feel this way about me? How did my other cousin know my name without me telling him? I started to remember other cousins who said that they would watch me from a distance. What was it about me that intrigued them? Were my family and I people that my hundreds of relatives watched from a distance all these years? Were they all told and warned by the bishops to remember my parents and shun them for life? Were we relatives who crossed over the line of religion into a world of which they could never be a part? I wondered, *Do they, in their minds, cross over that line and wish they could in real life be free, like me? My heritage*, I thought, *under so much bondage. Don't they know Jesus Christ has come to set us free?*

After the burial, all the mourners went back to the house for a meal together. Daddy didn't want to go, so he said his good-byes at the graveyard. He told them we had a long drive home, and he wanted to be home before dark, so we left. We got something to eat on the way home.

CHAPTER 29

Shunned for Life

That is why, for Christ's sake, I delight in weaknesses,
in insults, in hardships, in persecutions, in difficulties.
For when I am weak, then I am strong.

2 CORINTHIANS 12:10

IT WASN'T UNTIL SEVEN YEARS later that I fully understood what really went on at the meal. As a child I remember staying for the meal, but it really didn't mean much to me except that I finally got to eat after sitting through the long funeral and then waiting so long after the burial. Now I can understand why Daddy really didn't want to stay. He would have set himself up for rejection and hurt. The shunning! I don't think Daddy could have endured it so soon after Mother's death. You would think that after more than fifty years, the bishops would give up, but they have to keep the rules and the shunning for life.

My cousin Cathy's father died. Daddy went to the viewing to give his condolence to his sister Betty. While there, Cathy asked him to make sure that he let me know about the funeral and to see if I could come.

Daddy called me and asked if I would take him to the funeral. I really didn't want to, but knew I had to for him. He would have to go by himself if I didn't take him. Heaviness came upon me. The same heavy feeling came upon me when I had to go to Amish funerals as a child. The worst of it was that I had to sit all by myself. Daddy reiterated that they asked specifically for me to come. I couldn't understand why, but I knew that Daddy would appreciate it if I would go. I liked to visit them, but I really didn't want to go to the funeral. I had gone to one seven years ago, and that was enough. I remembered the feeling of being out of place and different. I didn't care to go through that again.

The morning of the funeral, I tried to dress very simply and wore a plain, dark, navy-blue dress. It was a hot summer day, so I put on my navy sandals. I slipped off one set of earrings, thinking they wouldn't notice my little diamond studs and I could just leave them in. After putting on some lipstick, I thought maybe it was a little too much, so I didn't put on any other makeup. I would be as plain as possible. Not fussing with my hair, I let it have a natural look. As I was walking out the door, I felt I better take another pair of shoes just in case I shouldn't wear sandals. I really didn't know if that would offend them.

When I picked up my dad I asked, "Daddy, should I change anything I am wearing before I get there? Do I need to take off my rings, watch, or bracelets? Oh, do I need to put on different shoes?"

He said, "No. I am keeping my watch and ring on. You look fine."

"Are my shoes all right?" I asked. Then I noticed something that was not all right. My French pedicure. Then I also noticed the French manicure. Wow, I was in big trouble. So I slipped off my sandals and put on my shoes. I decided that was the best I could do for now and Daddy said, "Naomi, don't worry about it. No matter what you do, everything is wrong." But I didn't want to offend. How could I not offend? *I guess by not going,* I thought. I really didn't want to go. No matter how hard I tried to be plain, it really wouldn't work anyway.

My heart was pounding as Daddy and I walked to the front door. Everything was quiet on this hot sunny day, except my heart. I wanted to turn around and go back to my car, but we were now committed. A man came to the door and asked Daddy in Dutch who he was, and Daddy said, "Betty's breedah [Betty's brother]."

He then looked at me and asked my father, "Veah is de frau mit dich [Who is that lady with you]?"

Daddy said, "My madel [My daughter]."

He told Daddy to follow him and told me to wait. Oh, how I wanted to sit beside my daddy. How I wanted to hang on to him like I hung on to Mom when I was a child. I wanted to hide under his arm. As an adult, I still had the same childish feelings, feeling so out of place, wondering what they were thinking of me.

The man came back and led me, all by myself, to the room where the family was. I was sort of surprised. At first I thought, "Why is he putting me in here? There is a lot of space in that back room. There were less people in that room." Then a shocking thought came. I was family, wasn't I? I saw the cousin who asked me to come sitting close by, but we didn't make eye contact.

Strange feelings of discomfort engulfed me when I saw all their plain colorless faces. I bit my red lips as we walked in so no one could see the fiery lipstick color. It probably wasn't that outstanding, but any color on my face I'm sure was noticed. After I sat down, I took my Kleenex and tried to wipe my lips in a way that wouldn't reveal what I was really doing. I felt as though all eyes were on me. All I noticed was how different I was. I looked for a place to lean against. I wanted to hide. There was no place to go and no back to lean or rest against. This time I was all alone, even though right beside me was an Amish lady. Was she my cousin? Most likely she was. What was she thinking of me? She glanced at my hands. Then I noticed the four rings on my fingers. *Oh, Lord, what did I do? Why didn't I just take them all off?* Trying to hide my hands, I turned the rings around so the diamonds and sapphires were hidden in my palms. I clutched my hands to hide my painted fingernails.

How glad I was that I had changed my shoes. At least I didn't have to hide my toes also. I was feeling a little better when I noticed the thick black stockings all the women were wearing. I had bare, tanned legs. I pulled my dress to cover my ankles and tucked them under the bench. It just wouldn't stop. I saw an endless list of offenses.

In the stillness of the onlookers, I felt guilty as charged. Seeking relief, I thought of the passage about a woman who was to be stoned for committing adultery and heard Jesus say, "He who has no sin, cast the first stone." The people left one by one. Then Jesus looked at the women and asked, "Who is here to condemn you?"

"No one," she replied.

"Then neither do I condemn you," He said.

I felt the Lord comforting and rescuing me from a falsely accusing mind.

As the silent waiting continued, I observed some more convicting traditions that once again pricked my soul. I realized my head was not covered. That was a big one. My mother always made sure she had her head covered when she went to visit them. Why didn't I think of it? I could have grabbed something to put on my head. I also wore navy blue, and every woman there had on black. Black as could be. I had a black dress at home. I had forgotten that women wear black and that men wear dark navy blue. One would think I would have learned this by now. Why didn't I wear black?

Doesn't it say in the Bible that man looks at the outward appearance, but the Lord looks at the heart? It was then that I finally thought to myself, *Lord, forgive me if I would offend anyone here. You know my heart and You know that I didn't want to offend anyone. Lord, You are the only One that matters to me. My intention was to dress so I would not offend anyone. Daddy was right. No matter what I wore, everything was wrong, but Lord I love You and I love these people; help them to see something special in me. Help them see You in me.*

The man who was leading people in and telling them where to sit brought in a family and had them sit on the porch. They were ex-Amish. They are people who once joined the Amish church but then left the Amish religion. This family dressed plain. The women wore head coverings, but they were not dressed like the Amish. The pressure was off of me, and I felt a little better. I wasn't the only different person there. I sort of relaxed a little.

The funeral started and relieved my mind and got me thinking about what the bishops were saying. Trying to understand was next to impossible. I had been away from the language too long. I could only understand bits and pieces. I wanted so much to understand what they were saying. The Amish bishops and preachers speak "high" German at funerals and church services. The people speak Dutch, "low" German, all the time. At one time the Amish were only allowed to own German Bibles. Now the bishops and preachers use them and preach from the German, but the people are now allowed to own English Bibles in their homes. But that depends on the sect and community of Amish. Each sect has different rules about which Bible they may use.

Time went by fast, but it did not go fast enough, for I really had a desire to get away to go home or at least be by my daddy. I always felt safe next to him. Glancing across the room, I saw him sitting with his two brothers. I felt fondness. Here was deep love, more than I could ever express to him. He saved me from all this. He paid a high price for my freedom. The sad part was that he was still paying for it, and he was eighty-six years old. For more than fifty years he had put up with persecution and so many difficulties, yet he always stayed strong.

After the burial at the graveyard, we were walking to our cars to go back to the house for the meal. Daddy stopped and talked to the couple who were ex-Amish and had moved away from the area. Daddy asked them a question about what the bishop said at the funeral. Daddy seemed concerned that they not be hurt by the accusations that the bishops made. They reassured him they weren't hurt and said they understood why the bishop had to say what he did.

"Are you staying for the meal?" I asked them, hoping someone who wasn't Amish would be there so we wouldn't be alone.

"Oh, no, we have to head home," they said.

I knew Daddy wanted to stay for the meal and be with his family, and I really did want to see my cousin also. Dad and I had stopped in to see them a few times, and I also took her shopping one time. I wanted to let her know I cared. What I didn't know was that I was about to experience first-hand what my parents experienced almost their whole lives.

I questioned Daddy about the comment the bishop made about the ex-Amish. He said, "Oh, those bishops just have to do their job, keep the tradition. In his sermon he told us, the ones who left the Amish, 'You broke your promise that you made on your knees before God and the church. By breaking that promise you took it under your own feet and walked all over it. It doesn't mean anything to you. You are responsible for your actions!'"

Then Daddy in his own calm way chuckled and said, "The vow I made on my knees was to obey their rules and never leave the Amish Church. I might have said it, but it didn't mean anything to me. It was something that all the Amish have to say when they are baptized. Then when you are baptized, you automatically become a member of the Amish Church. Yes, I am responsible for the vow I made before God. I should have never said it. They made me say it. I did sin when I broke that promise, but I asked Someone greater, Who can take away my sin and wipe it away forever, I asked Jesus, and He forgave me, and I live free from bondage!"

My daddy had the strength to stand firm when those all around him thought he was wrong. How could he be so faithful all these years? He never wavered, even in the hard times. I felt guilty in just the few hours I was around them. Would I have been able to remain a part of their lives like my parents had? It would have been easier to leave and not visit them again—or would it?

Reminded of the guilt I felt back at the funeral, I took off more of my jewelry and placed it in the car ashtray. I didn't want to have to hide it when we were eating at the meal.

We drove up to the house where all the Amish were outside waiting for the meal. It seemed all eyes were on Daddy and me as we drove up. It didn't help that I had a shiny, brand-new Sebring limited edition convertible. Once again I felt out of place. I did not want to stop. I wanted to drive right past, but we were committed. I thought, *No wonder the bishops have to put the ex-Amish in their place. They have to keep their flock from being tempted to stray into the world's ways.*

Walking up to the house, I saw that all the men were together in a group and all the women were in a group. *Now, where do I go?* I thought. I didn't want to go to the ladies. I didn't know any of them. So I stayed by Daddy. After a while I started feeling out of place, and I walked over to the ladies, but they didn't talk to me. I wished the ex-Amish family had stayed. I finally saw my aunt who had also left the Amish, but she dressed and looked just like the Amish. I couldn't tell a difference. I walked over to her, and we talked a while.

They called for all the aunts to file in to eat. I said to my aunt, "What should I do?"

She took my hand and said, "You just stay with me." We started to walk up to the house. Then my aunt said, "Oh, I need to go to the bathroom first before we go in and eat." So we went to the other house and used the bathroom. There were three houses close together all in the same area.

After we were done, we came out and saw that the uncles had also gone in to eat, and Daddy and my uncle, my aunt's husband, were still standing outside. We walked over to them and they said that the others had gone in, but they were told to stay outside.

At the meal, the immediate family eats first. Then the aunts or sisters of the deceased person file in, then after the women are done eating, the uncles or brothers go in and eat. They go in and eat and then leave so the next group can go in. Women and men eat at separate tables. Then the first cousins go in and eat. Then the rest of the relatives and friends go last.

We sat under a tree with a nice breeze blowing through the branches. We waited for the shifts to change and for someone to come out and tell us to come in and eat, but no one did. Daddy looked at me and said, "Do you want to leave and get something to eat in town?" I think Daddy was feeling a little uncomfortable for me.

I said, "No, my cousin asked me to come, and I would like to talk to her."

As we waited in the hot sun, I felt an overwhelming sense of rejection. Not feeling welcome is one thing, but this was worse, much worse. It was as though they lured you to a place and then deserted you. It seemed clear they didn't want us around. Or was it the fear of what the bishops would do if they didn't shun us? Maybe the family did want us there.

How could Daddy and my mother put up with this nonsense all these years? I felt myself pull my body closer to Daddy and found myself wanting to crawl under his arm and hide. It was like a flashback to when I was a little girl, not wanting to be with these strange people and hiding behind my mother's arms.

Not only did I feel uncomfortable that day, I also felt embarrassment for my Amish relatives having to act so foolish. I also felt a need to voice my opinion to people who think the Amish lifestyle is wonderful. They believe a lie. Some people look in and are intrigued, longing for a simple way of life with tranquility. You see it all over: Amish pictures with Bible verses portraying a holy, righteous sect. I hear it all the time: "Amish life must be wonderful." You know, I also am almost lured into believing the lie, but I had a taste of both worlds my whole life.

After most people were fed, nine ladies came toward us. Four of the ladies handed us each a tray with food on it. The other four gave us pie and a drink. One of the other ladies asked if anyone wanted coffee. As soon as they were there, they were gone. Daddy said a prayer and we began to eat.

Daddy in all his wisdom and optimism said, "Look at this: we got served really good food. We didn't even have to go and get it ourselves. Here we are out under this nice tree with a cool breeze. We didn't have to eat in the house where it is hot. Isn't that nice?"

What does it feel like to be shunned? Well, I got a taste of it only once, and it wasn't a nice feeling. Would I have endured a lifetime of this? Was it worth it? Obviously my father and mother thought so.

My cousin never came to talk to me. I had to go to her. Daddy said, "If she had come to you, the bishops would have had to talk to her. It was all right for you to go to her."

Thankfulness welled up inside me for my parents. My father was a rebellious, unhappy Amish man. My mother was a strong-willed Amish woman who didn't want to leave her religion, yet she loved and was committed to her rebellious husband. God changed both of their hearts, and they became committed to the Lord and to each other. With God, they became strong. They chose to endure a lifetime of hardships, persecution, and broken relationships for Christ's sake. Together they became God's perfect team who set our family free.

CHAPTER 30

The Calling

*Being confident of this, that he who began a good
work in you will carry it on to completion until the
day of Christ Jesus.*

PHILIPPIANS 1:6

MY MOTHER WAS CONFIDENT THAT when she died she
was going to heaven. Growing up she had been taught that you
could not know for sure if you were going to heaven. If you think
you are going to heaven, you are a proud person. You could only
hope that you would be good enough for heaven; that is, you
might have a chance if you kept the Ordnung. Mom's life verse
was Philippians 1:6: "Being confident of this, that he who began
a good work in you will carry it on to completion."

God was still at work in my mother's life, even when she
looked like she was worthless. He took an old woman who was
an invalid and used her. She was blind, paralyzed, broken-down,
and lying helpless in a dreaded nursing-home bed for seven years.
He used her in her silent years of her life to tell a story to her
daughter to carry out His plan.

A neighbor, who was my mother's Home Health Care nurse for the ten months Daddy took care of her in his home, came to see us the evening Mother passed away. We were talking and she said, "I never thought she would live longer than a year after her brain hemorrhage, let alone for all these years. But sometimes, something needs to be done before one can be released to die."

"What do you mean?" I asked.

"I mean sometimes the person who is dying has a need to see a loved one they haven't seen in a long time. They strive to hang on to life until they see that loved one. Maybe they can't die when a certain person is around, like a child they want to protect from the pain of seeing a loved one die. Sometimes something just has to be accomplished before they can release themselves to die, like a prayer being answered."

I was taken aback, moved. I had never heard of this before, but it started to make me think. Some of those tucked-away memories started to surface.

During the sandwiched years of taking care of a growing, energetic teenage family and also caring for the concerns of my elderly parents, I became Area Representative for a Stonecroft Ministry's Christian Women's Club. It was a way for me to get involved with something to take my mind off the stressful things in my life. One of the responsibilities of the Area Representative was to teach women to tell their life stories.

In order to teach it, we had to learn by doing our own life story. The previous Area Representative encouraged me to write my own and present my speech in front of the Regional Representative to be critiqued. I wrote and presented my speech in the spring of 1994. When I was through, the Regional Representative said, "Now, when can you start speaking? Can we put you on our speaker's list now?" It all happened so fast. I was happy they liked my life story, but I really didn't feel that I should become a speaker.

Just ask my husband, Doyle, or any one of my children. I would say things like, "If you would like the cornbread a little warmer, just put it in the refrigerator for a little bit," or "Dinner is in the dishwasher." Now, how could I become a speaker? I struggled with my ability to be a speaker, yet inside I sort of wanted to do it. But I wasn't going to do anything unless it was what God planned for my life. I've had many disappointments, and I knew if it was not His plan for me, I would fail.

It was after I had written and sung the song for my mother that I made plans to record an album. It was one of my life dreams. I thought I'd start singing, buy a sound system, take a few music courses and voice lessons, and start my career.

I went to Cincinnati to record my album. As I was singing, the producer said to me, "Naomi, if you don't shape up, your background vocalists are going to sound better than you." I couldn't believe this was happening to me. They recorded the musicians, and I was stuck with the low range. I have a soprano voice, and it was very difficult for me to sing. I did it, but it wasn't me. I was totally disappointed.

As a child I had sung solos in my school and in churches. In high school, I knew that turning down the music scholarship was one of the biggest mistakes of my life, but my parents had insisted. The second blunder was totally making a botch of my solo in a big Christmas concert at church. I was embarrassed, humiliated, and felt like a complete failure. After that, people would still ask me to sing, but it wasn't the same. I was insecure, unsure of my abilities.

It all came to a head one day when I went to a new church and tried out for the adult choir. I had intended to tell the new music director that I sang solos, but I didn't feel I did well in my audition, so I left never mentioning it. I realized then that singing might not be what God was calling me to do. He said I was accepted into the choir, but I walked out defeated and I labeled myself a failure. I was broken.

Hurt and pain entered my being, and I wanted to die as all my failures from the past surfaced like bleeding, raw flesh. Thinking my wounds were all healed, I was devastated to find ripped-open wounds, and I now had another injury worse than the ones before.

Sobbing into my pillow, I hoped Doyle didn't hear my cry. I silently slipped out of bed, found a secluded place, and laid out all my hurts to God as I wept.

Lord, I do not understand. I have felt what I believed to be a calling all my life, and I thought it would be in a music ministry. Obviously it is not your calling for me. So, Lord, I will be content in what I know you have first called me to do right now and that is being a wife and a mother. Nothing more! Nothing less! I give you all my hurts, my failures, and my broken dreams. I put them in the past. Please take them from me. Heal me. Restore me. I surrender!

Broken, I began to pick up the pieces of my life, handing them to God and trusting that somehow he would put me back together and make me whole. As the tears subsided, I had peace and was beginning to believe that He knew what was best for me; I just had to let my broken dreams be repaired by God and pray His plans for my life would become my passion.

When a lady called to set a speaking date, I hesitated. I just could not make the commitment. I was weak and afraid. I was afraid of failing again.

The lady could tell I was not ready to speak on the date she requested, so she asked, "When would you like to speak?"

"I would like to sometime in the new year." I thought six months was a long way off, and it would be a great way to start out a new year. I could cope with that. So she booked me way in advance. I booked my first two speaking engagements, one on Monday, January 9, 1995, and the second on Tuesday, January 10, 1995. For six months calls came in for me to speak. I had booked twenty-three engagements in the year of 1995, all before I even started to speak.

January came too soon and I became very nervous, but I knew I had to do it. I could not back out now. The first time I spoke, my legs were shaking. I was nervous and afraid, but I knew if this was what God called me to do, He would help me through. As I got into my speech, I felt some relief. I could stand still and feel more at ease. I began to relax. Then I felt the joy of completion, knowing He had definitely helped me.

After the brunch a lady came to me and asked, "Do you speak for mother and daughter banquets?"

"Well, no," I said, surprised. "This is the first time I ever spoke." She didn't care and asked if I would consider doing the banquet for them in May. I was excited because I would have a lot to say about my dear mother. She had been speaking to me in her silence for the past seven years. I loved the idea and got excited about the opportunity.

Slowly fear entered my being. *I really can't do this*, I thought. I started to have doubts about my ability to write another speech. That first speech did not come easily for me. *I cannot write, I cannot spell, and I never was good with grammar in school. How can I do this?* Explaining the situation to Doyle, he reassured me that computers do all that for you now. But I still have problems with spelling and grammar because grammar and spell-check sometimes can't even recognize what I am trying to say.

The following day I spoke again at another Christian Women's Club luncheon with a little more confidence, knowing I could do this with God's help. Joy filled my heart, and love overflowed for the One Who has helped me through it all. I was even beginning to like speaking.

Right after I got home from speaking at the second luncheon, there was a message on my answering machine saying my mother had turned for the worse. I called them back, and her nurse said that they didn't expect her to live.

For once I had felt like the storm was subsiding and the waves were gently flowing back and forth on the beautiful, peaceful, sandy shore. I was happy from speaking and having a good time at the luncheon when suddenly, out of nowhere, a gushing wind erupts, causing a wave to crash against the rocks. Now, I was heartsick hearing the sad news about my mom. It was a familiar uneasy feeling that I had felt many times over the past years, and it was not a comfortable one.

The next day I packed my bags and planned to stay by my mother's side. I canceled appointments and made arrangements for my children.

I spoke for the first time on Monday, January 9, 1995. The second time was January 10, 1995. Two days later on January 12, 1995, my mother died. The wonder of it all is that the first time I spoke a lady asked me if I would speak at a mother and daughter banquet. "Sometimes, something needs to be done before one can be released to die."

The phrase "you must become broken before you can be useful" started to make sense. Does God care about a daughter's failures and broken dreams? Does God care about the hardships and cries of a brokenhearted, broken-down mother? Did God really hear my mother's cry many years ago in a small, old house in my parents' bedroom for her child to be a preacher?

Why did Mom want her daughter to be a preacher anyway?

I may not be a preacher like the one at the revival meetings that Mom and Dad attended so many years ago, but I feel the call, the passion, as did my mother, to proclaim the mighty truth: "Being confident of this, that he who began a good work in you will carry it on to completion until the day of Christ Jesus" (Philippians 1:6).

CHAPTER 31

Dorothy's Secret

So we fix our eyes not on what is seen, but on what
is unseen, since what is seen is temporary, but what is
unseen is eternal.

2 CORINTHIANS 4:18

SOMETHING WAS GOING ON IN the house because Mom
and Dad were scurrying around very intensely. I wanted to see what
was going on, but I was sent out to play and told not to come back
in until I was told to. I walked up and down the sidewalk kick-
ing whatever foreign object was in my path. I still had my Sunday
clothes on, so I couldn't climb the trees or play like I would if I
had on an everyday dress; Mom would get very frustrated with
me if I tore my Sunday dress. I wanted to change my clothes, but
they wouldn't even let me in to do that. So I just kept walking
and playing nicely with my dog and cat. I wondered what was
so important that I couldn't be in the house with the rest of the
family. I knew something was wrong, but what?

That Sunday was a mystery that stayed with me even until
my adult years. Somehow even as I am writing this, I never asked

my family what went on that day. Now as I gather thoughts of the past and remember some tucked-away memories of certain conversations, I have come to my own conclusion.

One conversation was with my sister Dorothy. I was staying with her at her apartment for a few days, and some boys came over to visit her. One of the boys was interested in me and asked Dorothy if he could take me out. I was in my early teens and Dorothy was very reluctant to let me be alone with this guy. He was older, more Dorothy's age, and I heard her tell him, "You can if you don't touch her."

Before he came to pick me up the next day, Dorothy set me down and told me something no one had ever told me. She said, "When I was a young teenager, I got pregnant, and then I had a miscarriage. It was a very humiliating time for me and I don't want any of that to ever happen to you. Now this guy wants to take you out, but don't you ever let him touch you. Do you hear me? Never let boys touch you until you are married!"

I never forgot what my sweet sister confided in and counseled me on that day. It was short and to the point. I got the gist of her message, and I didn't have to ask any more questions. Now, I wish I would have asked more questions, but then I heard all I needed to hear. I could tell she was deeply hurt by that big tragedy and loved me enough to tell me her failure so it would never happen to me.

Something happened between Dorothy and our parents that none of us really knows. It must have been so dramatic for her back then, because she left home and no one knew where she was. We went years without hearing from her. I do remember once she did come home for only a short stay. She was sick and sleeping in the living room. I would get the things she needed, and I loved being by her. I don't know why, but she soon left home again.

No one knew where she lived, where she worked, or if she was dead or alive.

She came back into our lives when she was in her twenties and living with my sister Kathy, who was married. Later on she moved out and got an apartment with some friends in the same area.

Dorothy got married, and I wish I could say she lived happily ever after, but that was not planned for her. The married couple lived in Ohio for some years and then moved to Arizona, where her husband left her. My oldest brother Atlee owned a restaurant there, and Kathy moved there to help out. Dorothy worked for Atlee also but always lived an unfortunate life. A couple of times her home was broken into and was robbed of the little she owned.

In the midst of all her trials, if we tried to talk to her about Jesus, she would say, "Don't talk to me about Jesus. I know all about Him, and I want no part with it."

I don't think she really knew Jesus; she only knew what a religion did to her. She also knew people who professed to know Him, but because of a stressful situation she felt she was treated with disrespect, and maybe she was. She couldn't separate the two, Jesus and religion, because as a young girl that hurt was branded deep on her heart that she would "never amount to anything." I believe that haunted her most of her life.

One day at the restaurant, a couple who had been regular customers asked Dorothy to go to church with them.

"I can't go because I don't have a car." She gladly gave the excuse.

"We'll pick you up," the couple insisted.

Dorothy was never the same after that encounter with that couple. Whatever happened, she made an about-face. Jesus, Whom she had never wanted to talk about, became her on-going topic of conversation. Jesus became very precious to her. He became so precious that she found ways to put Jesus in her crafts, letters, cards, on key chains, walls, and everywhere else she could find a place.

She was so excited about her new life that she told everyone about it. The one person she wanted most to tell could not comprehend. Mom was then in the nursing home and could not remember the present, only the past. Dorothy visited her and told her the good news, but Mom in her frail mind could not really grasp her news or all her joy. Dorothy actually became depressed and had counseling for the disappointment of never having her mother rejoice with her. Dorothy knew all the heartache she had caused her parents and wanted to reconcile with her mother.

Going back to the scene at the casket with Dorothy crying over Mom, I believe Mom had gone to Dorothy in the past and asked for forgiveness for hurting her and Dorothy probably wouldn't accept her forgiveness. When Dorothy's heart changed she wanted to go to Mom and ask Mom to forgive her and accept Mom's forgiveness, but that never happened.

Dorothy soon found comfort in knowing that she would spend eternity in heaven with Mother and that was all that mattered. I had one conversation with Dorothy in which she said, "I wish I can be the first one in heaven to tell Mom, because in heaven Mom will understand."

Three years after Mother passed away, Dorothy got the dreaded news that she had cancer. She battled that deadly illness for two years, always hanging on to Jesus no matter how horrible the pain.

My sister Betty and I were by her bedside one morning while she was in hospice care. We were listening to a tape of praise music Betty had brought for her to listen to. I slept in the room with Dorothy all night, and Betty came in to relieve me. For some reason I couldn't leave.

Betty prompted me off and on, "Naomi, come on. Go get ready. I want to get some coffee."

"I just can't leave. I don't know why, but I can't." I was wondering what was keeping me from leaving the room.

Dorothy was sitting propped up with pillows and was not responding to Betty or me if we asked her questions. So Betty and I just kept on with conversation trying to include Dorothy, but we didn't get a response even though she was wide awake. This was the first that she had not talked to us. Betty asked her to squeeze her hand. She didn't, but she did pick up her hand and pointed to the bulletin board that had some cards hanging on it.

"Nice cards, aren't they Dorothy?" Betty said.

Dorothy didn't say a word but then pointed to her eyes and then pointed to the bulletin board again.

"She is trying to tell us something. But why isn't she talking to us?" I asked.

This went on for about half an hour. We knew she was seeing things that we could not see, but what was it? Betty and I could not figure out what she wanted us to see. A couple of times she pointed to the ceiling.

Betty prompted me again to get ready so she could get some coffee, but neither of us could leave. I even told Betty she could leave and get her coffee and come back, but she couldn't leave either.

It was then that our dear sister lifted her arms straight up toward heaven, her eyes opened wide, looking up, as the sweet praises of the music filled the hushed room. She held her arms there for a few seconds and then her arms went limp and fell to her side. Her head slumped and a horrible noise erupted. Nothing Betty and I had ever heard before came bursting from her lifeless body. The noise was so loud that the nurse came running in asking us if we wanted to leave. "You don't have to leave, but you can if you want."

Betty and I didn't know what in the world had just happened. "What is going on?" we asked the nurse.

"Patients do that sometimes," she replied, never really explaining as she franticly moved Dorothy to her side and used the suction pump to remove fluid. "Why don't you go and get some coffee if you want."

Betty and I were on our way down the stairs when the nurse came after us and said, "I'm sorry, but your sister just passed away. She died right after you left. Go have your breakfast and we'll clean her up so you can be with her when you get back."

Betty and I sat at breakfast knowing something supernatural had happened that morning. We finally determined that

Dorothy saw something, and it was not the bulletin board or the ceiling that she wanted us to see. We don't know who it was; maybe it was an angel, maybe Jesus, maybe Mom. Whoever it was, we know she wanted them, for she eagerly reached out for them. Her spirit lifted from her earthly body, leaving it limp as it screamed out thunderous death rattles. Her body struggled for breath, but it was too late. She was set free and was flying to her new home in heaven.

Dorothy was born into eternal life October 20, 2000, at the age of fifty-seven. She may have gotten her wish to be the first to tell Mother she was saved.

Can you know for sure you are going to heaven, or can you only hope? When you die, will you be able to reach out and be born into eternal life in heaven? Or will you die a fearful death? You can know for sure you are going to heaven.

Betty and I know for sure Dorothy is there. It was the unseen Holy Spirit there in her room keeping us from leaving. Why? For the reason that God guarantees eternal life for those who believe in His Son, Jesus. He is the Healer of broken lives, and He wanted us to witness it so that we can proclaim the mighty truth that God is still changing lives. God continues to work in and care for the simple, the empty, and the broken down.

If you do not know Jesus, here are some facts. God loved us so much that He sent His only begotten Son, Jesus, to redeem us. He was born of a virgin, He lived as a man on this earth, He was crucified and died on the cross to save us from our sins, and He was buried. After three days, the awesome, mighty power of God had victory over the sting of death and He rose victoriously from the dead. He ascended into heaven and sits at the right-hand side of God.

Now anyone can know these facts. Dorothy knew all about Him but wanted nothing to do with Him. Knowing facts about Him is not enough to get you to heaven, but the miracle is that you can have a *personal* relationship with Him and He will save you from the sting of death. Dorothy's whole attitude and life changed, and she became a different, happy, fulfilled, joyful person.

Oh, loved ones. Please make this prayer your own:

Dear God,

Thank You for sending Your Son Jesus to die on the cross as a way of paying the penalty for my sins. I believe that You did raise Jesus from the dead. I accept Your Son Jesus as my personal Savior. Thank You that I can know that You have forgiven me and that I am now a new person, a child of God.

In Jesus' precious name, Amen.

If you let Jesus capture your heart, He will change your life forever!

CHAPTER 32

Trip Home

Christ Jesus came into the world to save sinners—
of whom I am the worst. But for that very reason I
was shown mercy so that in me, the worst of sinners,
Christ Jesus might display his immense patience as
an example for those who would believe in him and
receive eternal life.

1 TIMOTHY 1:15B–16

A PALLBEARER IS ONE WHO helps carry their loved one's coffin to their final rest. Never, but never, would I have thought that some day I would be taking my sister's remains home to Ohio with me on a plane for her final resting place. Dorothy wanted to be buried by Mom, and someone told her that if she was cremated she could be buried on top of Mom's grave. It would be a much cheaper way to transfer her body from Arizona to Ohio. We carried out her wishes, and I was chosen to be the bearer.

The funeral director gave me Dorothy's remains and said everything I needed was included. Her ashes were in a box and the box was placed in a nice bag. I took the bag, placed it in a larger cloth bag with handles, took a soft gray shawl, and placed it around the box.

Checking in at the airport, I asked, "My sister was cremated, and I have her remains with me now. Is there anything special I need to do?"

"No, just go through security. They will take care of everything," the ticket agent said.

Walking up to security was very awkward for me. I thought, *Should I put her on the conveyor belt or walk up and hand her to one of the security guards?* With all the people in line I finally decided to put her on the conveyor belt. Well, when she went through the x-ray inspection, it seemed like all the lights and beepers went off. I don't remember if the lights and beepers really went off or not, but my heart was pounding when everything came to a screeching halt.

The security guard shouted, "What do you have in here?"

"My sister's remains," I replied timidly, as everything around me came to a sudden silence and all eyes were on me.

"What?" the guard shouted. "What did you say?"

I stepped closer and sort of whispered again, "It's my sister's remains."

"Your sister's remains?" Still not understanding.

"Yes, my sister was cremated, and I am taking her remains home." By then everyone was moving closer to hear this unusual conversation.

"Well, you have to step aside and be checked."

They took me off to the side and asked, "Do you have her death certificate? You know you need her death certificate!"

"I don't know. The funeral director said I had everything I needed to fly home. I know I don't have it. It must be and I hope it's in the bag."

They took everything apart and inspected the whole bag. Thankfully they found the death certificate on the bottom of the bag and let me proceed to the plane.

There I found my seat next to the window. A gentleman was already sitting in the aisle seat. He let me in. As I sat down, I placed Dorothy's remains under the seat in front of me. The plane was full, but there was still an empty seat next to me and some behind me. I settled back and watched the movement outside as attendants checked seatbelts and helped passengers. Right when I thought that no one else was getting on the plane and thought that I might have an empty seat next to me, a bunch of men entered the plane and came my way.

One of the men stopped by our row, looked at the seat numbers, and stepped over the gentleman in the aisle seat. As he was coming in to sit down beside me, he looked me right in the eyes, and his first words to me were, "Meeting me may change your life forever."

Startled from his comment, I said nothing.

"How are you? My name is John. What's yours?" he asked.

"Naomi," I said and nothing more. I was hoping that he would settle down, leave me alone, and talk to the gentleman next to him. No such luck. He talked excitedly, and I finally joined in on the conversation that lasted the whole five hours on that non-stop plane ride home. We started talking about our marriages.

"I won't let my wife do anything for me," he said as he informed me that he might be getting a divorce when he gets back home.

"Why won't you let your wife do anything for you?" I asked.

"Because I won't let anyone do anything for me. I don't want to *owe* anyone anything."

"Give me an example?" I asked.

"Well, like I won't let her give me a back rub."

"Will you give your wife a back rub?

"Oh yes, but I won't let her give me one. I told you, I will not let anyone do anything for me, but I can do things for them."

"No wonder you are ready for a divorce. To have a happy marriage you have to give and *take*, not just give."

"Well, I just can't. I've always been this way. I can't and don't want to accept anything from anybody."

There was a moment of silence for my heart was pounding, prompting me to say what was on my mind. I didn't want to, but I knew I had to. So I sat up in my seat, leaned against the window, looked at him, and said assuredly, "You are going to have to accept something someday if you ever want to get into heaven."

"What do you mean?" he asked.

"I mean if you want to go to heaven, you have to accept Jesus Christ as your Savior. He is the only way to get into heaven. Without Him you are lost forever."

"I don't want anything to do with religion."

"You don't have to do anything with religion. I said Jesus. You need to have a relationship with Jesus."

"Well, I don't want to give anything up."

"What don't you want to give up?"

"Smoking! I just don't ever want to give it up. I tried; I can't stop. Plus I like it."

Once again there was a moment of silence as my heart pounded, prompting me to say something I thought I would never say. I prayed silently. *Lord, is this thought from you? If it is, let it flow from my mouth. If it's not from You, hold my tongue.*

As soon as that prayer was done, out from my mouth flowed, "My sister Dorothy smoked, and I know she went to heaven."

"Did I hear you right? Your sister smoked, and you *know* she's in heaven? How do you *know* she's in heaven?" he asked, surprised.

I told him the wonderful story of the amazing minutes just before my sister's death. As I told him the story, I could tell he was softening and ready to listen. I concluded, "God takes you as you are and then changes your life when you are ready. You don't have to give up anything to receive Jesus as your Savior. Dorothy struggled about her smoking. It was bad for her health and she knew it. She smoked a lot less, but she just couldn't stop completely. God knew her heart, and all I know is that she's in heaven."

"You're really sure about that?"

"Yes, I am, and do you know she's here on this plane right now?"

"No, what do you mean?"

"Dorothy was cremated just a few weeks ago, and I am taking her remains home. There she is, down there in that bag under the seat.

His mouth dropped in amazement and he asked, "Are you really telling the truth?"

"Yes. Look!" I uncovered the gray shawl around her box and also showed him the death certificate. We had a few laughs when I told him all about the excitement with the airport security. I took out a Creative Memories album that I made while I stayed in Arizona and showed him pictures of her. He became interested in my family and looked at the whole album.

After we were done looking at the album, he brought up the subject again. "Well, I don't know all about that religion stuff. There are so many religions, how do you know which one is right?" he asked.

"I don't get concerned about names of religions. Jesus said, 'I am the way, the truth, and the life. No one comes to the Father except through me.' Jesus' name is in the Bible, but nowhere in the Bible can you find the names of churches like Methodist, Lutheran, Amish, Mennonite, or Catholic. The list could go on, but you know what I mean. You have to seek out a church where the main thing is Jesus Christ. Ask God, and the Holy Spirit will lead you into all truth. He'll guide you to where you should worship Him," I explained.

He settled back and thought a moment and said, "Last night I was at a sales meeting conference. I went out to smoke and some guys came out and were trying to convert me. They were telling me all about their religion."

"What religion is it?" I asked.

"I think Christian Orthodox. Have you heard of it?"

Amazement filled me, knowing this encounter was also intended to comfort me. I had just heard about this religion, had questions, and did some research on my own. "Believe it or not my son-in-law just became an ordained deacon this past February. He is planning on becoming a priest. The Orthodox Christian Church says their roots trace directly back to the first-century Antioch, the city in which the disciples of Jesus Christ were first called Christians."

"Is that your religion?" he asked.

"No, but like I said, I don't get concerned about religions. Ask God to lead you to a church where the main focus is Jesus Christ and the teaching is truth from the Bible."

"Wow, I don't know what to say. These guys I work with have been inviting me to go with them to their church," he said.

"Just go with them. I've gone to an Orthodox church. My daughter and son-in-law were just converted over to that church, so check it out," I encouraged.

"They're here, right behind us," he said.

"Who's here?" I asked.

He turned and pointed to the man in the middle seat. "This is Mike, the guy trying to get me to go to his church. Oh, by the way, we're salesmen and we sell vitamins."

"Hi," Mike said. "I have been listening to your conversation and praying for you this whole trip."

God made an appointment for John and me to meet because God knew John needed to hear about Dorothy. That dear man could have had the seat behind me and this conversation would have never taken place.

We all three talked some more, and soon John got back to wondering how he could save his marriage. The whole five-hour-long trip had not one moment wasted.

This was the most amazing plane ride I have ever taken. It was not a coincidence that John got a seat next to me. The situation was perfect for John to meet Dorothy. He was willing to

listen to me because I didn't say you have to stop smoking to become a Christian. Dorothy thought that she would never amount
to anything and always felt defeated because of her smoking and
failures. But because of Dorothy's life, one more soul may go to
heaven. I could testify to John that God still changes lives by her
example. Believe me, God continues to work in and care for the
simple, the empty, and the broken down.

"By the way," John said, "when I first saw you I was planning
on selling you vitamins. How funny is that?" He paused and
then said, "Your husband sounds like a great guy. Do you think
your husband would mind if I met him?"

"He would love to meet you, and, yes, he is a great husband,"
I said with thankfulness in my heart. We had talked about our
marriages and I told him how my husband treats me.

"Naomi," he said, "I got on this plane saying to you that
meeting *me* may change your life forever. But meeting *you* may
have changed my life forever!"

I knew this encounter was planned by God.

We got off the airplane, and as we were walking to the gate I
saw Doyle smiling from ear to ear, holding a dozen yellow roses,
waiting to embrace me. I said, "John, that's Doyle, the one with
the roses."

"It is? He has *roses* for you?"

I introduced Doyle to John, and John said, "I hope you don't
mind, but I talked to your wife the whole trip. She told me a lot
about you and I just wanted to meet this great guy of hers."

With Doyle's expression of love to me, I knew he said it all,
and John walked away a new man.

CHAPTER 33

"Scrumptious!"

Yet I am always with you; you hold me by my right
hand. You guide me with your counsel, and afterward
you will take me into glory.

PSALM 73: 23–24

"DADDY, WE CAN'T GO AND visit all your brothers, because
some have passed away and some live far away. Bill lives in Florida,
Freeman lives about two hours away, and John we just visited
Friday," I explained, trying to figure out why all of a sudden this
became so important. It was Monday, about two in the afternoon,
and I was working around the house.

He got up from the recliner and walked toward the kitchen.

"Well, I just have to go and see my brothers!" he said, sitting
on a chair putting on his shoes then picking up his cane. "Come,
take me to see my brothers."

"Daddy, why do you have to go and see your brothers?" He
hadn't mentioned this ever before, and now in an instant, he was
insisting to leave right now. What in the world had popped into
his head?

"Because I have to tell them that I am going to die this week. I'm going home," he explained with urgency that I couldn't ignore and couldn't believe.

"Daddy, what in the world do you mean?"

"I mean I am going to die and I need to tell my brothers, so come on, let's go!"

I knew then that there was no convincing him that it was not true, and I had to come up with a plan to calm him, real quick.

"Daddy, what if we call them and you can talk to them, because it would be just too long of a drive to get to their homes this late in the day."

I could tell he wasn't real thrilled with the new idea, but he went along with it.

We were privileged to care for Daddy in our home, and he had been with us for about four weeks. We moved my office upstairs and moved Daddy into the small, cozy room with his bed, dresser, and comfy, worn-out favorite chair. He mostly stayed in the living room with us, reclining in my favorite chair. What a privilege to give up my favorite chair to my first love, my daddy. He was such a blessing to care for because he always had a smile on his face, answering, "Scrumptious!" when I asked him how he was in the morning.

Every day, at any time and out of nowhere, Daddy would say, "The blessings of the Lord are rich and there is no sorrow in them."

He had become real frail and we had visiting nurses coming into our home. I slipped away after Daddy called his brothers and called Home Health Care and told them that Daddy was saying he was going to die this week. The nurse told me to believe him and that they would send someone out right away from hospice care. I couldn't believe that they believed him. "Oh yes, sometimes people know that they are going to die and say when, so believe him."

"Really!" News to me; I had never heard of that before.

After Daddy talked to his brothers on the phone, he went to the bathroom and wanted to go to bed. I helped him and asked if he wanted anything to eat and he said no.

Well, of course I called my siblings right away and Betty came up the next morning.

The whole day Daddy did not eat or talk to us; he slept in bed all day. Betty spent the night. We checked on him during the night but he was just sleeping and we heard nothing from him all night. The next morning we didn't know what to expect. Both Betty and I went into his room together, and what do you know—we couldn't believe our eyes. Daddy was sitting up on the edge of his bed with a big smile on his face.

Shocked, we said, "Good morning! How are you?"

"Scrumptious!" he said with a delightful, ornery smile. He ate a little breakfast, slept some, and then after lunch he walked out to the living room. Betty went home around 7:30 p.m. because she thought everything was fine. That evening he could not get up out of the recliner and could not walk back to bed. Doyle and I helped him to bed and got him settled for the night. I got up during the night to check on him and he wanted a drink and said, "I don't understand what God's doing. I know I am going to die; I'm not fooling around."

Hospice care nurses came every day and by Thursday things had drastically changed. He no longer could get out of bed and had excruciating, unbearable pain. On Saturday a hospital bed was brought in, and it was horrible to see him in so much pain while they moved him. Still he didn't complain and only said encouraging words to the nurses.

The nurses were amazed with him. Word soon got out about him, and other nurses requested to be able to take the next call that was to take care of this Simon. They wanted to meet the Simon Mullet that everyone had been talking about.

Saturday night the hospice nurse said, "It will be soon, but your father told me he can't go because his two daughters, Kathy and Naomi, have not released him to go."

Kathy and I looked at each other and said, "What?"

"You two have to go and tell him that you will be all right and say goodbye to him," the nurse explained.

What a difficult thing to do—one I wanted to avoid. Kathy had flown in from Arizona that day and was spending the night. We just couldn't get ourselves together to go in and tell him that night. The nurse said, "He is settled in, but you need to put these pain pills in his mouth every three hours."

The nurse had told us that he was fine and all tucked in and to let him rest, so Betty, Kathy, Fred, and I went into the kitchen and were talking rather loudly. Daddy called for Fred to come into his room and said, "Tell those girls to quiet down; they are making too much noise." When Fred relayed the message, we all had a good chuckle.

We had a monitor in our bedroom so I could hear Daddy if he called me. My sleep was interrupted with any slight sounds, the alarm going off every three hours, thoughts, and grief. Around 6:00 a.m. I awoke franticly and jumped out of bed, thinking I had missed his pain medicine, but the alarm hadn't gone off yet. I hurried to his room and heard a hushed rhythmic murmur. I said, "Daddy, I have some pills I need you to take."

"I don't want any," he whispered.

"Well Daddy, they are for your pain. I will put one in the side of your mouth and it will dissolve, okay?"

He sweetly replied, "Thanks, honey."

After I placed the pill in his mouth, he continued his hushed rhythmic murmur almost like a mix between humming and singing.

"Daddy, I love you. You know I love you," I said as I held his hand. His hands, his strong hands, reminded me that we have no fear of the sting of death when we know Who is holding us in the palm of His hand.

"I know, honey. I love you too," he whispered, never opening his eyes.

"Daddy, it's all right for you to go," I said, tears streaming down my face, barely able to speak.

He squeezed my hand and said, "Thank you, honey, thank you."

I kissed his cheek. "I'll get Kathy, and I'll be right back."

Kathy went to her father, gave him her love, and also released him. We all gathered together to be by his side and each child gave him their love and said their goodbyes. Daddy was right. Six days after he announced that he was going to leave us for eternity in heaven, he took his last breath. He went to be with the Lord at noon on Sunday, June 13, 2004.

Daddy spent his last four hours on earth quietly singing, talking, and raising his arms toward heaven in constant communication with Jesus. He repeated over and over, "Thank You, Jesus, for all You have done for me. Thank You, Jesus, for saving me. Thank You, Jesus. . . ."

My daddy, the one who taught me all about my Heavenly Father by his life, not by his words, but simply by his life, has now taught me by his death.

There is no sting in death if I place my life in my Heavenly Father's hands!

CHAPTER 34

Cousin Encounters

Who may ascend the mountain of the Lord? Who may stand in his holy place? Such is the generation of those who seek him, who seek your face, God of Jacob.

PSALM 24:3, 6

MY HUSBAND WAS TAKING A client from work out on a tour of Amish country at the client's request. He was from Egypt and wanted to learn more about different religions in the United States. He was also a doctor, so we first took him to the Amish birthing center. We toured the facility, which is operated by Amish for only Amish mothers. Amish are not allowed to buy insurance, so to cut down on cost, they built their own birthing center. They have auctions during the year, and the area ladies made a cookbook for sale to raise money for the center.

We drove around the farmlands enjoying the beautiful scenery with horses and buggies slowly clip-clopping down the road. We saw children frolicking blissfully in the yards and flower gardens waving to us as we drove by. Clothes of plain color hung flowing in the breeze on clotheslines, strung from pole to pole.

Mothers were tending to their gardens or sitting on the porch snapping beans. Men were working in the fields, walking behind the horse-drawn plows.

Our second stop was at an Amish furniture store. We got out to look around, checking the beautiful handmade furniture with different kinds of wood, stains, and styles. We did not buy anything, but we ended up in a conversation with the owner. There was no one else in the store, so we were not holding him up. Being curious, I told him my parents' names. He right away lit up, saying my father Simon was his uncle, which made us first cousins. He knew my brother Fred.

"Yes, I know Fredie. I used to work with him," the cousin said.

We talked a while and decided to move on. As we left he gave us his business card and said, "Tell Fredie to come and see me sometime. Yah, I really like Fredie."

It was interesting to hear him call my brother Fredie. I didn't remember anybody calling him that, but I guess that must have been before my time.

Some of my friends wanted me to organize a dinner in an Amish home. Calling a few of my father's friends, I got a name and address of a couple in Burton Station who did such meals. She did not have a phone, so the only way you could get in touch with her was to stop by or write. Since we were in the area we decided to look her up.

We found the house where the Amish meals were cooked, but there were cars parked in their driveway and by the road, so we weren't sure. Looking into the porch, we saw a lot of people eating, and we decided that they must have been having a dinner at that time. I was reluctant about going in, but I knew it was the only way to make an appointment for a dinner. They must be used to strangers knocking on their door if they run a business and don't have phones.

It was a beautiful summer evening, still light outside, and the windows were open. I had to pass the kitchen window to get to the front door. As I passed, I noticed a lady washing dishes right by the open window. I looked in and said, "Hi, sorry to bother you now, but I was wondering if you cook meals for groups of people in your home."

"Yes, I do."

I paused a moment because I was taken aback by something though I didn't know quite what. I blurted out, "You look so familiar."

"I do? Come on in." She pointed to the front door as she wiped her hands on a towel.

I walked over to the door, and she let me in.

"If this is a bad time, I can come back or write," I said, apologizing.

"Oh, no! This is fine. The rush is over. The people are just visiting amongst themselves."

She gave me her business card and a few dates that she had open for dinners.

I took hold of the doorknob and was about to leave but just couldn't without saying again, "You look so familiar." To me it was even eerie. I knew she looked like someone I knew but just couldn't put my finger on it. Then I said something that always has given me a response: "My parents are Simon and Susan Mullet."

"Susan is my aunt. People say that I look like her," she said without hesitation.

Leaving her and walking out to the van, I was amazed that I had a first cousin that looked like my mother and I never knew her. I was excited about planning an event to be in her home and to get to know her better. I was also amazed that out of the three stops we made, I met two of my first cousins. It was not unusual for Daddy to say as I was taking him somewhere, "Your aunt lives at that place. Your cousin lives right beside her, and across the street is another cousin." After the impact of that evening, I came to believe that I was related to the whole town of Middlefield.

The family-style Amish wedding dinner in my cousin's home was exceptional. We had chicken, dressing, mashed potatoes, gravy, creamed peas, pickles, bread and jams, salad, two kinds of jell-o, three kinds of pie, date pudding, and coffee. Believe me, we were full. What a wonderful evening. It was kind of nice being with my cousin and having a taste of her delicious food and company. We relaxed, visited, saw similarities in our behavior, and laughed. Some family traits are naturally passed down from generation to generation; others you have to seek out.

While I was writing this book, there were so many times I just wanted to ask someone who was Amish a few questions. If you noticed, I had quite a few unanswered questions about how the Amish feel about us. I felt I couldn't ask an Amish person because I wasn't close enough to any to be able to ask such questions. So I wrote what my father told me, wondering if he was the only exception.

One Sunday I was talking to a friend at my church. Her mother was my father's aunt! So what does that make us? First cousins once removed? Her parents left the Amish around the same time my parents left. Actually, her father was a bishop in the Amish Church. A bishop leaving the church rarely happens. She informed me that I have a first cousin attending our church. About three thousand people attend the church, so it would be easy not to see them there.

I said, "Now you do know, most of my first cousins are Amish." (I was the only one not born Amish, on both sides of our family. Some of them have left over the years, and little by little some are still leaving.)

"Yes, I know. But she left about fifteen years ago. She also has cancer. You have to meet her. She is a cousin on your mother's side."

I was surprised because I don't hear of many leaving the strict Old Order.

One Sunday I was standing, waiting for a friend, and this small lady came up to me and said, "Are you Naomi?"

"Yes, I am."

"Hi, I'm Barb, your first cousin. This is my husband, Andy."

Talk about godsent. We hit it off right away, and what a blessing. They are the most beautiful couple. The love of the Lord just radiates from them. It feels like we have known them all our lives. They have been such an encouragement and help to me. God answered my prayer in sending them my way. They answered many of my questions about the Amish and have enriched my life.

My father passed away nine years after Mother died. He was eighty-eight years old. The morning he died, Barb and Andy were with us. It felt good to have them there; they were now family, family who cared.

At my father's funeral a man came up to me and said, "I hear you need a carpenter. I don't have any work right now and could use it."

Doyle and I had bought a farm and were in the process of restoring it. The house was ready for a finishing carpenter. A week before my father died, I took Dad to see his Amish brother. While we were there, an aunt and some cousins stopped in. I was telling them we were looking for a finish carpenter. One of the cousins told me her brother was looking for work. She must have passed on the information to her brother about the possibility of a job with us.

We set a date for him to come out and see if this job was something he wanted to do. My husband, Doyle, was taking bids and interviewing carpenters.

Joey drove up in a big Ford truck, and out jumped his white dog. Right away he won my heart. I love dogs. Doyle took him around, showing him what needed to be done in the house. He would say, "Yah, I think I could do that."

When he left we weren't sure about him. He was very different from the other contractors that gave us bids. Most contractors brag on how wonderful they are and that they could do most anything. We found out the hard way that they are mostly full of flattery. Joey didn't say anything about how good he was.

Doyle decided to have my cousin Joey do the work. He was a simple, single, rough and tough, strong guy who sort of looked like and reminded me of my dad. He had thick, tough, calloused hands just like my dad's, so of course this guy was special to me right away. Under his hardheaded mannerisms is a tender and kind heart that people could take advantage of if he let them. He was the kind of guy that would have done a handstand on top of a silo. When Joey was younger, his father had told him the story of my dad doing a handstand on top of a silo. So Joey asked if he could try, and his father would not let him.

Joey's family left the Amish religion when he was twelve years old. I had always heard my father refer to him as Joey. But when he started to work for us, he told me since his father had died, he was now Joe.

Uncle Joe knew a lot of stories about my dad. Growing up, they were partners in crime. When Uncle Will came to visit from Plain City, he stayed with Uncle Joe. They would reminisce old times, and as a little boy, Joe would listen, taking it all in.

Four months Joe worked for us full time. During those four months, I found out things I never knew about my father. Stories I added to this book. God knew I needed Joe, and he also knew that Joe needed us. Doyle and I heard pent-up feelings of hurt and pain that would make our heart ache. Unbelievable tales, only to find out they were true. They were stories that were kept inside for years, just waiting for a listening ear, for someone to understand and care. As each story heaved from his soul, there was healing. As he emptied out his heart of hurt and pain, the bond between us grew stronger and stronger.

Not only did we gain a great friend, but laughter began to fill the walls of our house. Our house started to become a home, and to our amazement, Joe did an outstanding job. The job was far better than we ever imagined or deserved. Joe was not an ordinary carpenter—he was a skilled craftsman. Doyle wanted to have the same woodwork that was in the original house. The wood was thicker than what you could buy in the stores today. Joe had rough-sawn oak that was perfect for our job stored in his barn, so he sold it to us. It was lots of work to get the rough boards ready to make into trim, move it, stack it, then plane all four sides many times. Move it, stack it, and put it through a sander many times. Move it, stack it . . . I think we handled each board about fifty times before it was ready for trim.

As much as we had, we still ran out of wood, so we had to locate a place that had wood like we were using. We went to Amish country and stopped at an Amish salvage food store. We looked around and got a few things. We told the man as we were checking out what kind of wood we were looking for and asked if he knew of a place we could get it.

"Oh, yes! Down the road, first street, turn left, and it's the second farm on the right."

We drove to the farm. There was no sign out front to indicate that there was a lumber shop, but we drove in anyway hoping we were at the right place. The shop was in the back, behind the house. Doyle went in to check it out, and I stayed in the car. About twenty minutes later he came out and asked me to come in because the man who owned the place was my first cousin on my mother's side and he wanted to meet me. By now I wasn't surprised.

My home is finished with wood from my first cousin on my father's side and my first cousin on my mother's side. Something I never thought would happen, and never dreamed could happen. What a blessing for us. Joe also had some special pieces of wood that he had saved over the years, and he gave them up; he used them in our house. We feel so blessed for his generosity. They hang in a special place, with love written all over them. I have learned from Joe that unique pieces of wood to carpenters are like beautiful material to quilters. You hang on to them because it's hard to cut into them. That is, until you find just the right home for them.

Joe was finished working in our home and packed up all his tools one Saturday evening. The next Monday morning, we heard he had been life-flighted to Metro Hospital Sunday evening and was in the burn unit. Joe had gotten all tangled up with a power takeoff shaft while working on his farm grinding corn. It ripped off almost all his skin down to the muscle on his right thigh.

Without going into details, Joe almost didn't make it while going through all the skin grafts, infections, fungus, and blood clots. He suffered for seven weeks in the hospital, and we thought we would lose him. Somehow God was not done with him and saved him, not only physically, but also spiritually. He has continual pain and a mean limp, but you don't hear him complain. He does say, "Boy, I really messed myself up!" He also says, "God had a reason to keep me alive."

One more life to proclaim the mighty truth that God is still changing lives, continuing to work through and care for the simple, the empty, and the broken down.

CHAPTER 35

Hidden Treasure

*Praise be to the God and Father of our Lord Jesus
Christ! In his great mercy he has given us new birth
into a living hope through the resurrection of Jesus
Christ from the dead, and into an inheritance that can
never perish, spoil or fade. This inheritance is kept
in heaven for you, who through faith are shielded by
God's power until the coming of the salvation that is
ready to be revealed in the last time.*

1 PETER 1:3–5

FRUSTRATED, I PUSHED THE KEYBOARD away. I laid my
head on my arms and sobbed with papers all around me on my
desk. I just could not go on. What made me think I could ever
write this book? I can't write! I never claimed I could. Why did
God give me a story if He is not going to equip me to do what
He asked me to do? Defeated, I cried out to God.

"God, I am going to put this book away. I am going to put it
on the shelf, and if you really want me to complete it, then you
will have to show me. I just cannot do this—I don't know how!"

I cleaned up my desk, saved what I had written on the computer, and powered it off. I sat back in my chair, stared at my clean desk, and thought what a sorry mess I was.

Suddenly the phone rang, and it was my friend Claire. She asked what I was doing, so I told her my dilemma. She said, "Naomi, if God really wants you to write this book, He will make it clear to you, and you will know when to take that book off the shelf and start writing again." She then asked, "Are you doing anything this morning?"

"No, my calendar just got cleared." I was feeling guilty because I had set goals and I was not accomplishing them. I had been working on writing the book for months, and it seemed like it was dragging on and I was getting nowhere. You could say I was a little discouraged. I knew I had a story to tell, but I am not a writer.

Claire said, "Let's go to a garage sale. There is one in town that has lots of quilt stuff advertised."

That's all I needed to hear. Maybe I just needed to get away. It lifted my spirits a little, and I felt sort of relieved. I got in my car and was on my way to pick her up. Claire and I were members of a quilt club, and we loved to find quilting bargains.

We got out of the car, and together we walked up to a table at the garage sale. We stood beside each other just looking at the stuff on the table, and I could not believe my eyes.

There was a quilt magazine lying right in front of us on the table, all by itself.

Shocked, I pointed to the magazine and said, "Claire, you won't believe this, but my mother's picture is in that magazine."

"No! How do you know?" she asked.

I picked up the March 1986 *Lady's Circle Patchwork Quilts* magazine and turned right to the page. There she was, sitting around a quilt with her friends from her quilt club. I knew my mother's picture was in that magazine because she had given me a copy when it was published years ago.

We both just stood there. I was still in shock. Claire was amazed. The unbelievable thing about this was that there was a whole stack of quilt magazines at the back of this table, but this one, and only this one, was lying all by itself right in front. It almost seemed like the magazine had come alive, crawled right out of the stack, and taken its place in plain view just for me to see.

Claire looked at me and said with assurance, "Naomi, you better take your book off the shelf and start writing again! I think you have your answer."

I couldn't believe what had just happened. God knew I needed my friend Claire with me because I don't think anyone would have believed me about the magazine had I not had a witness.

I have now written this book about my mother, and I can say it wasn't easy. Many times God would tell me with His gentle whispers, "Naomi, keep going; never give up. *My power is made perfect in your weakness.*" I guess God never really told me it would be easy, but one thing I know for sure is that He did help me, and I also know this for sure: I am compelled to tell this story.

My mother's love and compassion was evident the moment she had a relationship with Jesus. She felt the amazing change in her heart and knew it was real. It was a benchmark, a milestone in her life. The laws that bound her were released, and she was free to reunite with her husband after shunning him. I was the result of that union. As a child I always wondered why I had to go with them to all the Amish funerals. I wondered why Mom would proudly introduce me, as if she were announcing to the Amish, "See, she is the visible result of our being set free." As I write this book, I am stirred by the thought that my mother was proud I represented that benchmark in their lives.

My mother received a handkerchief that probably wiped away the very tears that were shed for her. She was the "wayward daughter." A religion tore a mother and daughter apart. How wounded she must have been to be labeled the wayward daughter all her life. But God, in His goodness, gave a story to me, her daughter, and answered my mother's prayer, proclaiming the mighty truth that God still cared for someone who seemed worthless and broken.

When my mother received the basket of broken dishes, her family meant to hurt her, to let her know she made the wrong decision in leaving her family and religion. Hidden inside that basket of broken dishes was a treasure, an inheritance of eternal life in heaven. Someday it will be revealed in front of her whole family, and when that Last Will and Testament is read, my mother will not be excluded, because she is an heir, a child of the King! For in the Bible it says, "Everyone who has left houses or brothers or sisters or father or mother or wife or children or fields for my sake will receive a hundred times as much and will inherit eternal life" (Matthew 19:29). God would rather that we have a broken, repentant heart than obey man-made laws.

Ironic, isn't it? Mother received a basket of broken dishes for her inheritance because she left the Amish religion, breaking a man-made law. The outcome of the situation is the reverse of what the bishops thought. They believe that when you die, if you are not buried Amish and wearing handmade clothes, you are doomed and cut off from God, regardless of what condition your heart is in. But the only thing that really matters is what God sees in our hearts. He doesn't look at what we wear or have. He looks in our hearts. It says in the Bible, "People look at the outward appearance, but the Lord looks at the heart" (1 Samuel 16:7).

My mother was willing to give up her earthly family and inheritance because she knew of the great value of the kingdom of heaven. She was willing to give it all up to gain eternity in heaven. Just when eternity seems to be almost at an end, it will start all over again. It will never end. In light of eternity, persecution, difficulties, and sickness here on earth are only momentary. That is, if you will inherit eternal life in heaven.

Mother had to make a life-changing choice. Both alternatives were heartbreaking. Sometimes the right way is the hardest thing to do in life, but the easy way is the wrong way and it always leads to destruction. It was hard, but Mother accepted those broken dishes because she knew of the great value hidden in them—of such great value that it was worth enduring a lifetime of brokenness for the sake of her inheritance, her heavenly reward.

Simon and daughter Naomi

Susan and daughter Naomi

The Mullet children
Left to Right:
Atlee, Dorothy, Betty, Naomi, Fred, and Kathyrene

For more information about
Naomi Mullet Stutzman
&
A Basketful of Broken Dishes
please visit:

www.NaomiMulletStutzman.com
NaomiMulletStutzman@gmail.com
www.facebook.com/Link2Naomi
@NaomiStutzman

For more information about
AMBASSADOR INTERNATIONAL
please visit:

www.ambassador-international.com
@AmbassadorIntl
www.facebook.com/AmbassadorIntl